The Cosmos of Design

ETH Zurich
Verlag der Buchhandlung Walther König

The Cosmos of Design
Exploring the Designer's Mind

Simon Kretz

for t. s.

7	Introduction: Researching design
11	A "theory from within"

1
13	Design as idea and test
14	Using and testing ideas
16	Process or creative act?
21	The iterative cycle of design
24	Analysis or synthesis?
27	Design both finds and invents potentials and resources

2
31	Design as examination
32	Design as a means to acquiring insight
36	Problem areas of design
38	Design as qualitative-heuristic experimentation
40	The rationalization of the existing
46	Abduction
49	The specific abduction form of design

3
57	Design as experience
59	Repertoires as experiential products of design
64	Repertoires as stimuli for design

4
71	Design as theory of practice
74	The primacy of realization
77	Open-ended abduction and induction: thematization and typification
81	Flexible patterns as encyclopedic vehicles
85	Models as tools for re-concretization

93	Synopsis: The Cosmos of Design
94	The specific iteration form of design
97	The Cosmos of Design: an overview
102	The performativity of the Cosmos of Design
107	Bibliography & List of illustrations

Introduction:
Researching design

Not only about the moon, but also about the whole firmament the human mind created a vivid fantasy. It probably took a long time to structure the wide starry sky, and to develop a coherent system within a chaotic reality [...] Instead of a set of facts, knowledge referred to a set of constellations derived from perception [...] The firmament was filled with figures and images, such as the Orion, Castor and Pollux, the Great Bear, and others.

O.M. Ungers, 1981

Design is a creative act – and more. This book wishes to demonstrate that an entire cognitive cosmos grows out of design.

Design is first and foremost the imagining of a possible future, and thus reality can be altered through design. Design is therefore the locus of sensual production, where the leading idea and imaginings are applied and tested, gradually taking shape and developing creative power in the process.

Design is namely more than vision and idea. Design also means experimentation. With the goal of examining existing reality and thus being able to better comprehend it, design not only solves obvious problems, but is also used to challenge the existing reality. Problems often only even become visible through design. Design is thus not only a shaping force, but a seeking and inquiring activity. In this regard, the goal of design is new insights, new knowledge.

Furthermore, design rearranges the existing knowledge of reality and creates new contexts of meaning. Although every specific situation designers face is of course unique and consequently calls for individual consideration, design operations are also based on experience. Design does not start in a vacuum, but instead makes use of the given circumstances and develops them further. This is one of the great potentials of design: in order to create something new and unique, and thus examine and solve specific problems in concrete situations, handed down forms are both adopted and applied, as well as disrupted and suspended for innovative thought.

To summarize, the following can be said: in design, reality is altered, examined and reorganized. This book explores design along these three dimensions of *changing*, *examination* and *ordering* and opens up the broad *Cosmos of Design* in the process. The central thesis of this book should thus show that design can be viewed as the source of three interrelated dimensions: as an instrument of change, a means for gaining insight and a resource for a structuring of practical theory.

Simple examples are used for this purpose. Step by step, design thought processes are illuminated in four chapters building upon one another to drill down into the cognitive processes and patterns of thought. The focus here is on those central characteristics of design that usually occur unconsciously: speculative thought, cognition-oriented experimentation, iterative loops and abductive conclusions. They will all be traced in detail. In this process, the intuitive, random and imaginative aspects of design should under no circumstances be neglected but instead be understood and appreciated.

Shining the spotlight on design should help us understand design thought processes as an autonomous form of knowledge creation which we can interlink to other paths to insight. However, no attempt is made here to separate practice, research and theory from one another.[1] Instead, the focus will be on attempting to bind together the various dimensions through the elementary act of design and allowing them to cross-pollinate. Instead of sinking into fatal and indeed insurmountable divisions and scientific turf battles, the deeper patterns of thought, such as heuristics and empiricism, are presented in a relationship of mutual dependence and married with one another. Behind this intention lies the ideal of a project for knowledge creation across disciplines[2] where speculative and critical thinking exponentiate one another and in which design plays a key role.[3]

A "theory from within"

The American design theoretician, Donald Schön, formulated the task of researching design as a cognitive theory of that practice that lies implicitly concealed in artistic and intuitive processes that designers use to master situations of uncertainty, instability, uniqueness and inconsistency.[4] For this reason, (my own) considerations of the practicalities of designers and design teams serve as background material here, which I was able to compile over ten years of practical and research experience in the architecture department at ETH Zurich. These considerations will be presented in the course of the book, successively ordered and linked with one another. This results in a coherent concept of design thought processes: a theory of practice.[5]

It should be emphasized in this context that the *Cosmos of Design* is not to be viewed as providing instructions for action,

1 The three dimensions of design (changing, examination and ordering), which provide the central theme of this book, correspond more or less precisely with these three areas (practice, research and theory).
2 For definitions of the terms interdisciplinarity, multidisciplinarity and transdisciplinarity, see Balsiger 2005.
3 See Ungers 1982: 7–11.

4 Schön 1983: 49.
5 The heuristic thinker, Gerhard Kleining, formulated a vivid description of such an examination of practical thought and cognitive processes: "I have thus attempted to formulate a qualitative methodology that passes on the essence of that which I experienced in the context of my own activities in a comprehensible form as a set of instructions for self-research [...] and systematizes the process of discovery". (Kleining, in Witt

as in a book of methods, but instead as a description of design thought processes. Here the cosmos will be developed from the interior of design. This is therefore not an "external" theory that attempts to explain a phenomenon purely contemplatively but is instead an "internal" theory: a product of active doing, of gradual understanding and comparative ordering. Theoretical statement and practical application of design thought processes are mutually dependent and refer to one another.

The *Cosmos of Design* is based on many outstanding representations, observations and insights that illuminate design – in particular on the reflections of Donald Schön, who, to an extent, provided the preliminary structure for this work. This book now connects the many perspectives on the cognitive potential of design, so that the most varied bodies of knowledge revolving around design that exist can be compiled and situated. What is presented here is a systematic representation of the thought and cognitive processes of design, an explanatory model. The goal of the model is to improve the understanding of design, to provide a theoretical basis and to finally make it applicable for everyday design practice and teaching. This model will be developed over the course of the book and then merged to form a whole in the synopsis. Finally, the last chapter of the book reflects on the advantages and possible impacts of the explanatory model.

2004: 25) In keeping with this credo, the *Cosmos of Design* will not be presented as an undisputed, ontological fact but will nonetheless be structured as the most realistic totality possible – as a "provisional realization of a checkered assemblage" (Latour 2007: 359).

I
Design as idea and test

Using and testing ideas

In his influential book, *The Reflective Practitioner*, the philosopher and design theoretician, Donald Schön, describes architectural and urban planning design as a process of cyclical actions.[6] Each design action can be understood as an operation that simultaneously uses and tests a concept or idea. This operation results in both design projects and new insights and ideas. These new ideas can then in turn be used and tested in the course of further design actions. According to Schön, this results in a repeating process, a circle of seeking and finding.[7]

A simple example from the design course serves to illustrate this pattern of thought: let us assume that a hotel complex is to be designed on a south-facing slope at the seaside. (Figure 1)

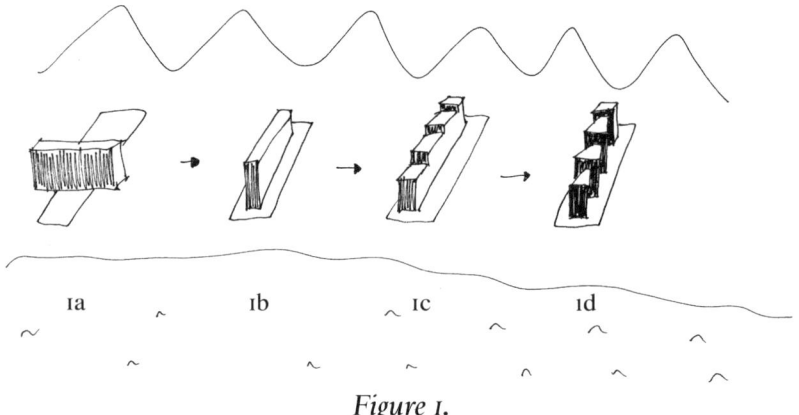

Figure 1.
Example of a hotel design

As an overriding idea, the architecture student imagines aligning all hotel rooms such that they face the sea, so that all guests can enjoy the breath-taking ocean view from their balconies. This initial idea originates from an imagining, an idea in which the ocean is the central element. It stimulates the initial design sketch: A simple slab facing the sea. In this way, all hotel rooms should offer an ocean view. (Figure 1a) The design idea can now be evaluated. The student notices that the hotel slab exceeds the boundaries of the given plot of land. The available

6 Schön 1983: 79–93.
7 Ibid

plot is unfortunately aligned transverse with the beach, but the designed hotel lateral with it. The student is now confronted with a choice. She will either attempt to alter the geometry of the plot or, since the plot is in fact aligned orthogonally with the beach and cannot be changed, evaluate the slab as not being realizable. Because the plot allocation in our example is interpreted by the designer as an impossible undertaking, the designing of a slab thus does not appear to be expedient. The first design sketch has failed. As a reaction to this, the student turns the building by 90 degrees, so that the hotel no longer exceeds the boundaries of the plot. (Figure 1b) This application is now in line with building laws, but does not agree with the design idea, as only a few hotel rooms offer an ocean view. The overriding idea of the ocean view can now either be abandoned or retained. The student in our example does not wish to give up so easily. The idea of the ocean view is important to her. She stands firm and opts for the latter. The idea shaping the design is thus provisionally retained for further tests. As the next application, the roof of the structure is adapted to the slope and graduated. (Figure 1c) This provides more rooms with the desired ocean view, but not all of them. The student now remembers a building she had toured several years ago on an excursion, where the architect had quite elegantly solved a similar problem with rooms arranged in a fan shape. This flash of insight hits like a bolt of lightning. A solution is suddenly within reach. The fan-like approach is used, and look: with a façade designed with a pronged shape, a view of the ocean is possible from every room, and the building is still contained within the prescribed plot of land. (Figure 1d) The many design loops paid off for the student; a promising building form was found.

It can be summarized that the concept or the design idea, intended to equip all hotel rooms with a balcony facing the ocean, is used and tested in the course of several actions. Each action forms a transformation that represents a difference from the previous attempt and can thus also be evaluated accordingly. The result of the test serves respectively as the starting point or instruction for action for the next attempt. The conception of simultaneous use and testing described by the example differs from the explanatory models, which conceptualize the design as a linear sequence of individual actions along a predetermined path or which subdivide the design process into phases of analysis and synthesis.[8] In contrast with this, when designing, Schön presumes a unit of thought and action that cannot be subdivided any further, which transformatively manufactures a difference from that existing in an open field of possibility and evaluates this at the same time.[9] Looking back at Schön, this operation was also designated as a "use/test-entity".[10] If one pursues Schön's thought further, a series of such operations results in an iterative process in which on the one hand designs are successively optimized, while the applied theses, theories or "leading ideas"[11] are tested in the specific situation for their potential realization. In the example of the hotel design, the step-by-step optimization corresponds with the gradual formation of a volume, which should, if possible, enable all hotel rooms a window facing the ocean. The test of the "leading idea" used leads to the recognition that a plot is available in the encountered situation that makes the design of a simple slab impossible. Only following various volumetric stratagems does it become possible to conciliate the design idea and the specific situation with one another. The process of design is thus at the same time a mediation between idea and situation, between needs and reality and between sensual perception and ordering logic.

Process or creative act?

The architect and theoretician, Christian Gänshirt, contextualized Schön's notion by differentiating between two fundamental approaches to explaining design. On the one hand processual design theories and on the other explanatory approaches that represent design as an individual creative act.[12] Both explanatory approaches can be found in the example of the hotel design, depending on the perspective taken.

In the case of processual explanatory approaches, design is understood more as "developing"[13], which requires a lot of

8   See Alexander 1971.
9   Schön 1983: 85.
10 Gedenryd 1998: 81–86.
11 Dewey 1927b: 8.
12 Gänshirt 2011: 64–78.
13 Mies van der Rohe, in Blaser 1977: 14.

time. This involves an "iterative procedure of generating and restricting variety"[14], in which various options are systematically developed and compared. The respective best option is pursued and points the way to the next phase. The architect, Hans Kollhoff, describes this variant-based design, which he credits to his teacher Oswald Mathias Ungers, as follows:

> First, you mark off the horizon, consider everything that might be possible, get quite carried away in the process and [...] also think of things that initially appear to be absurd. From this, you then develop a typology with variants, which you once again discuss and whittle down. Most of it ends up in the trash basket. In this way, several alternatives crystallize, which are then examined [...] and pursued in depth.[15]

Mathematician and physicist Horst Rittel envisaged this development of a solution using variants as a path. This path is not always simple and straightforward, but instead often progresses in loops and spiral movements, not seldom ending in dead ends.[16] (Figure 2) According to this explanatory model, the specific, individual and new arises here through the multiplicity of images, plans and strategies that are worked through in the development process, and which make every situation involving action a choice and a decision. In the process, both logical path dependencies and sometimes even inexplicable coincidences are considered parts of the process.[17]

This systematic approach contrasts with the explanatory approach that is convinced that the process of design is not a paced-out path of decisions, but is instead intuitive and proceeds simultaneously and often with unforeseeable, chaotic quantum leaps.[18] Here, "all knowledge and skill comes together at once", and designers are "present as a full person, with all their senses, all their abilities, all their experience and all of their cultural characteristics".[19] As a consequence, the individual act of creation can neither be subdivided into individual steps nor be logically itemized, in marked contrast with the concept of the processual explanatory approach. The explanation of design as an individual act is based on the writings of practicing architects

14 Rittel 1992: 75.
15 Kollhoff 2018: 162. When otherwise not stated all quotes cited from original non-English language sources without official translation have been translated into English by Kenneth Friend.
16 Rittel 1992: 75, McLuhan 1964: 49–50.
17 See Fezer 2009.
18 Gänshirt 2011: 70.
19 Ibid: 78.

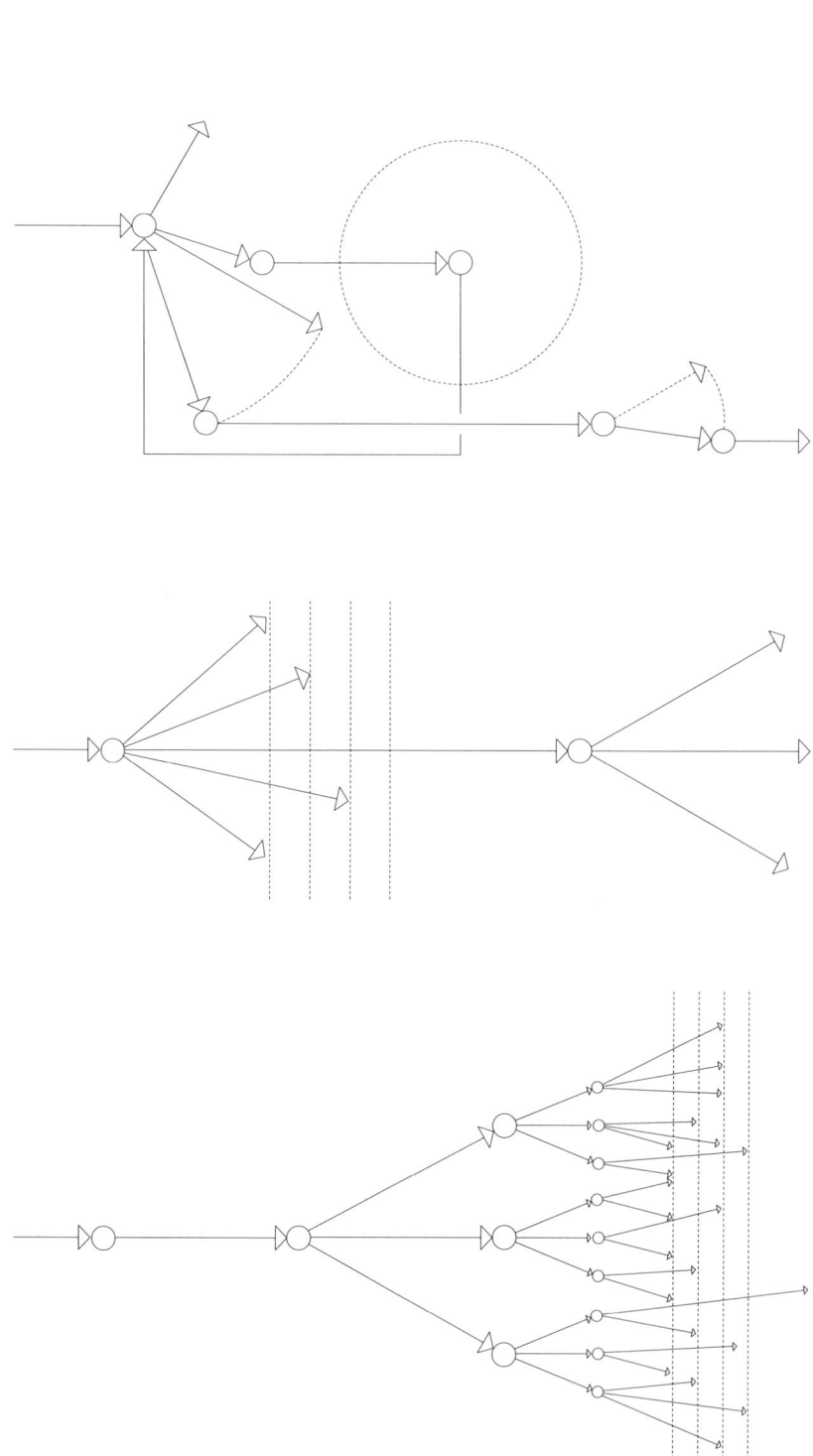

Figure 2.
Design as a process (Rittel 1992)

like Bruno Taut, who describes the slow shift in design from "thinking" to "feeling" in a wonderfully poetic fashion in his *Architekturlehre* [Teachings of Architecture], which was written in Japan:

> Everything is fine in practical and technical terms; there is nothing at all to object to. Ultimately, however, one begins to feel that five or ten centimeters to the right or left here and there [...] as well as other "trivialities" do nothing to change the fact that the thing remains just as practical and just as technically correct. [...] One places tracing paper over the drawings and the hand continues to draw – the head has approved it. [...] In order to elevate the solid and respectable to such an art, something else must be added. It is that difficult to define something that only concentrated feeling can bring.[20]

This explanatory approach, which understands design as an individual creative act, is also echoed in the now already canonical findings of the neurosciences, which involve the processing of the information provided by perception and memory.[21] In this research tradition, it has been found that far-sighted, anticipatory action mainly takes place intuitively and emotionally.[22] This also applies to design.[23] Because many different aspects must merge together under a real and specific circumstance to become a sensible total form, and because imaginative, new and unique aspects arise in the process, the synthetic decisions of the networking fireworks in the brain are not founded on a logical-analytical basis.[24] The high degree of complexity, the horizontal organization and the immense speed of this mental process make this impossible.[25] Design, conceived of as planning and acting ahead, is thus a highly intuitive, creative and emotional activity that cannot be analytically subdivided any further. Taut's "feeling", this "difficult to define something that only concentrated feeling can bring", is thus an emotional moment in design, which grows out of the logical paths of rational thinking and leaves these, at least temporarily.[26]

In her article on the perspectives of the architectural-philosophical research of design architect and philosopher Sabine Ammon wrote that both these explanatory approaches described

---

20 Taut [1935/36] 2009: 46–47.
21 See deBono 1970. This involves the differentiation of logical-analytical and intuitive-creative thought processes and their reflection in the organization of the two halves of the brain, which are asymmetrically structured in their weighting between networking structures running vertically and laterally with the cerebral cortex.
22 The reason for this are the neuronal networks progressing lateral to the cerebral cortex, which promote a comparatively weakly hierarchized agglomeration of various aspects of knowledge. They enable emotional assessments that deal holistically with the totality of a situation.
23 Toda 1980: 133–155, Pfister and Böhm 2008: 5–17, see Damasio 1994, 1999, 2010. The openness, the dependence upon context and the contingency that characterize planning tasks make routine or the following of familiar routine impossible. Quite the contrary, such decisions must be

above illuminate aspects of design, but are not productive in their pure form.[27] Neither the processual nor the intuitive explanatory approach deduce the essence of design in its entirety.

On the one hand, the explanation of design as an individual creative act attempts to spare the act of design a precise examination. In order to achieve this, it is claimed that design involves an inaccessible, intuitive and spontaneous act.[28] However, what is not expressed with this explanatory approach are the complex experiences and broadly branching thoughts that have prepared the unexplainable act and the difficult negotiation processes involved in finding a functioning solution that follows from this. This mystification makes insights into the origination of the design thought, reflection on the somnambulistic flash of insight of design itself and insights into the formative potency for the further development and realization of the same impossible. In Ammon's eyes, this explanatory approach tends to be unnecessarily glorifying.

On the other hand, Ammon believes that with the purely processual design explanations design is approximated with a uniform scientific process. Thus, attempts have been made to legitimize complex problem analyses, and the search for a solution based on objectifying criteria has been declared plausible. "In this manifestation of design research, the focus is on normatively oriented improvements and their tools in order to achieve an optimization of the process through methodologization and systematization".[29] In the process, the idea that coincidences, creative synthesis, emotional action, sensitivity and intuition are indeed relevant aspects of design is completely lost. This explanatory approach is oversimplified and provides little clarification.

Ammon determines that both explanatory models come up short as a consequence and are also often counter-productive because they stand in the way of a deeper comprehension of the actual practices of design as a result of their dialectical dispositions.[30]

made pre-reflectively as holistic emotions. And precisely these cognitive impulses that concern emotional activity cannot be conclusively comprehended rationally. That is the thesis of this explanatory approach, which conceives of design as an intuitive action.
24 In this context, particularly the lateral brain activity is meant, not the vertical.
25 Only in the aftermath, thus in the reflexive consideration of the design, can justifiable arguments and logical dependencies be named, and this too only to explain the result, but not to fully illuminate the creative act itself.
26 See Merleau-Ponty 1966, Johnson 1987, List 2009.
27 Ammon 2015: 185.
28 Ibid: 185, see Nerdinger 2003.
29 Ammon 2015: 185.
30 Ibid

The iterative cycle of design

Gänshirt reaches a similar conclusion and determines that it is actually both of the familiar explanatory concepts of design, meaning both processual and simultaneous concepts, that provide the basis for the fundamental cycle of three recurring actions: Here, this involves the iterative relationship of the three actions of *perception* (or also "critique"), *imagination* (or also "interior idea") and *expression* (or also "exterior representation").[31] (Figure 3)

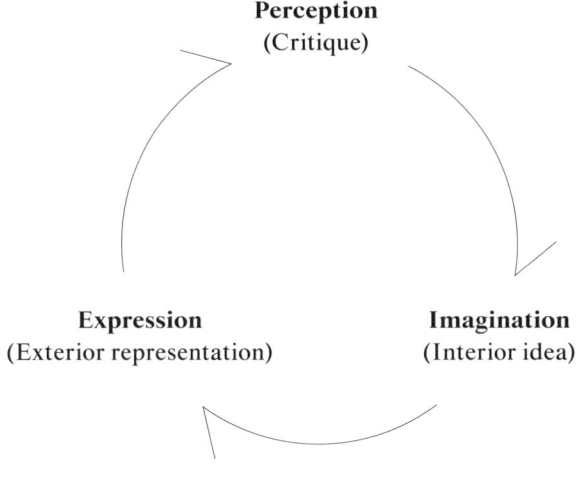

Figure 3.
Design as a cycle (Gänshirt 2011)

To illustrate this conceptualization, we look once again to the example of the hotel design: first, the geographical starting position of the student is acknowledged, whereby the location at the seaside is shown to be the most important characteristic. From this emerges the idea that all hotel rooms should allow a panoramic view of the ocean. This interior idea is provided with its initial representational expression in the sketch of the simple slab, which is aligned parallel with the coast. The drawn slab is thus an exterior representation, which is in turn perceived as a hypothetical future and criticized because the slab

31 Gänshirt 2011: 80.

is inappropriate for the plot layout. This critique now reflexively changes the student's interior idea which she later expresses in the form of a pronged and terraced building structure. (Figure 1, a–d) These new building forms are consequently the exterior representations of the altered interior idea. As the example shows, designing results in a cycle. This cycle is realized through the constant and in some cases simultaneously occurring repetition of the fundamental actions of perception, imagining and representation.[32]

However, the failed attempt at the simple slab parallel with the beach changes not only the subsequent design process, but also the student's perception. This changes because, due to the new positioning of the hotel perpendicular with the coastline, the pine forest, which climbs up the slope along the plot and now surrounds the rotated hotel, is suddenly perceived. This new attention devoted to the pine forest may be a coincidence but can also be ascribed to the rotation of the hotel. The rotation of the hotel in fact geometrically directs the focus to the downward sloping properties of the plot and thus allows the pine forest to appear in a relevant way, or to even shift into the focus of the always selective perception. The student's interior idea is in turn altered by the fact that she no longer simply wishes to design a hotel with an ocean view, but instead a hotel with an ocean view in the sparse pine forest. This changed idea will of course also heavily impact the subsequent design. For instance, small windows overlooking the pine forest will feature in the hotel rooms in addition to the large panorama windows with an ocean view – meaning the pines swaying gently in the breeze and the partially shaded forest floor, wafting of pine cones, can also be enjoyed. The emergence of the pine forest first shows that flashes of insight, unforeseeable events and ideas substantially influence design and that there is no logical decision-making path that one can stubbornly advance along from start to finish. In this example, however, it primarily becomes apparent that it is precisely the retroactive consideration of the externalization of an interior idea that helps the student to position herself in a reflexive relationship with this externalization relating to her

32 When one inserts the time axis into the cycle model, a metaphorical spiral emerges.

design and to herself. Not only possible futures and existing realities are examined in the design process, but also, in the broadest possible sense, perceptions and self-perceptions. The philosopher and anthropologist, Helmuth Plessner, described this dual perspective of entanglement with the term "eccentric positionality"[33], in which action and idea continually change one another and designers also perceive themselves through design.[34] The ability to see oneself in one's own images, drawings, models and ideas, to thus make oneself the object, is the special characteristic of this "eccentric positionality", which Plessner holds to be constitutive of the human life form, and which becomes apparent in its most expressive form when creating drafts and designing.[35]

With the complementary concept of "eccentric positionality", the circular thought model consisting of perception, imagination and representation can also be interpreted as a recourse to and expansion of the famous concept of the Italian architect and theoretician of the late Renaissance, Vincenzo Scamozzi: Designing is consequently understood as the externalization of an interior idea in the sense of a *Scientia speculativa*[36] [speculative science], as a *Scientia fattiva*[37] [active science] aimed at exterior representation and realization and as a reflexive form of self-perception and perception of the world, a *Scientia reflectiva* [reflexive science], so to speak.

With Schön too, reflection on an executed operation becomes a central function, as is already announced by the title of the book, *The Reflective Practitioner*.[38] His concept of design as simultaneous use and testing calls for the consideration of one's own design. According to Schön, the cognitive processing of the testing begins with this consideration. New, previously unknown questions and themes arise from this, which lead to new examinations. These new themes and questions can either lead to alternative design concepts, which can in turn be used and tested, or they are used to enrich and enhance the existing design idea.

33 See Plessner 1928.
34 See Schön 1992.
35 List 2009: 321, see Plessner [1928] 1975.
36 Scamozzi 1615: 5.
37 Ibid: 11.
38 See Schön 1983.

Analysis or synthesis?

When one pursues Schön's concept of the "use/test-entity" further, analysis and synthesis can initially not be separated from one another during design operations.[39] However, the separation of analysis and synthesis is possible reflexively. In retrospect, for example, the analysis of the plot geometry for the hotel design can be presented first, in order to then make a pitch for the terraced building as an elegant solution. However, as made apparent when discussing design creation, this usually does not correspond with the actual progression of the design. With the subdivision into analysis and synthesis, and this is the crux of the matter, it is not two phases of a process that are differentiated, as is often assumed, but instead two aspects of an operation that are illuminated.

The iterative cycle of design, which arises over the course of several such operations, can in retrospect be represented as a logical sequence of empirical analysis and creative synthesis processes. Such a simplification may be communicatively valuable but is strictly speaking not permissible. Design can be much better understood as a simultaneous, open and inventive search in a diffuse space of possibilities, which demonstrates both analytical and synthetic aspects.[40] The philosopher Friedrich Schleiermacher names the two poles of this open search as follows: "Inventing", which, in his opinion, often remains fatally disregarded, and the "found", which places knowledge in a logical context. "The art of inventing wants to become science, and the science of the found to become art, and the highest perfection is only reached in the identity of both".[41] The concept of interlocking art and science has a long tradition, particularly in the theory of architecture. Vitruvius was its founder, Alberti its greatest innovator.[42] This notion was shaken in the wake of the modern scientific era of the Enlightenment and at the latest by the momentous disciplinary differentiation which occurred in the early 20th century. Contexts of discovery and reasoning were separated from one another and creative "inventing" was split away from the systematic ordering of what was "found". While "inventing" itself was left to the arts and other creative disciplines, the examination

39 Gedenryd 1998: 18–68, 94–97.
40 The architect and urban planner Kees Christiaanse compares this course of events with simultaneous chess (Christiaanse et al. 2005: 149, see Hertzberger 1976) because the most varied disciplines and thought processes are at work at the same time here. Building on this, Christiaanse translates this pattern of thought into simultaneous, strategic concepts for urban planning projects (Christiaanse et al. 2005: 155).
41 Schleiermacher [1814] 1989: 5, see Klüsener 1998, Ungers 1982.
42 Vitruvius [approx. 33–22 B.C.] 1981: 13, see Alberti [approx. 1443–1452] 1485. In contemporary architectural discourse, this tradition of thought was reintroduced by the architectural theorists, Colin Rowe and Fred Koetter, with reference to the description of the "savage mind" of ethnologist Claude Lévi-Strauss (see Rowe and Koetter 1984; Lévi-Strauss 1962).

of cognitive processes was assigned to the disciplines of the social sciences and psychology. The justification of findings was in turn considered the task of philosophy.[42] Accordingly, the bond between the various directions of thought was severed in favor of the splitting of disciplines. Around a century after Schleiermacher, and as a reaction to splitting the disciplines in this way, the interlocking of art and science once again found a loud echo in the strategies of the modern avantgarde: no longer in such a self-explanatory manner as with Alberti or Vitruvius, but "aesthetic processes were objectified and scientific methods subjectivized" all the more instead.[44] It thus appeared as if not only a kinship existed between aesthetics and logic; a so-called "identicalness of methods" was even strived for.[45] The insight was that dividing attention, either between creative invention or scientific reasoning, suppresses precisely those issues of knowledge creation specifically posed in connection with design processes. In his theory of research, American philosopher and educator John Dewey also emphasized in 1938 that, for example, practices generating knowledge in medicine, engineering and physics demonstrated extensive parallels despite completely different results.[46] As a consequence, Dewey considered scientific, artistic and technical types of processes to be on an equal footing, and not in mutual opposition. In order to prove this, he identified experimentation as the central link:

There is absolutely no reason to draw a logical line between the operations and techniques of experimentation in the natural sciences and the same operations and techniques in favor of eminent practical goals. It is difficult to imagine anything more fatal to science than the elimination of experiments, and experimentation is a form of doing and making.[47]

As an example, Dewey describes an entirely practical activity: "The draining of swamps in which anopheles mosquitoes incubate is welcomed because it helps to eliminate malaria. However, from a scientific standpoint it is an experiment that confirms a theory".[48] Looking at Dewey's examination and at design as a practice, Ammon determines the following: "Where an unbridgeable gap between abstract formulas, long texts and buildings appears to

43   Ammon 2015: 186.
44   de Bruyn 2008: 71.
45   Giedion [1941] 1965: 40.
46   Dewey [1938] 2002: 504–505.
47   Ibid: 506.
48   Ibid: 505.

become manifest, a look at previous practices of experimentation and calculation, of interpretation and reaching conclusion, or simply of design, demonstrates astonishing similarities in their potential for generating knowledge".[49] Thus, the experimental process is firstly aimed at knowledge and is secondly probably the most interdisciplinary aspect in the fully differentiated and fragmented landscape of knowledge creation. This insight regarding the interlocked nature of finding and inventing among architects and artists, like that of scientific researchers and philosophers in the 20th century, is no isolated occurrence in the history of art and science, but instead applies across eras. This is especially apparent in the shared interest in experimentation and in other heuristic patterns. Examples of this are the theoretical treatments on heuristics of Albert Einstein and Ernst Mach, which are broadly familiar in the natural sciences.[50] Both deal in depth with the processes of finding and inventing that take place *prior to* the longed for and mostly suddenly occurring Eureka! moment. Here, not only are creative processes provoked, but existing contexts that sensitize and intensify the perception of specific characteristics are examined experimentally through genuine or conceptual alteration by means of experimental design.[51] Schön describes this process of simultaneous use and testing as follows:

[...] the practitioner allows himself to experience surprise, puzzlement, or confusion in a situation which he finds uncertain or unique. He reflects on the phenomenon before him, and on the prior understandings which have been implicit in his behavior. He carries out an experiment which serves to generate both a new understanding of the phenomenon and a change in the situation.[52]

Thus, the two dimensions, namely the changing dimension ("a change in the situation") and the examining dimension ("a new understanding of the phenomenon") not only refer to one another but are instead two dimensions of the same operation. To use the example of the hotel design again, both volume suggestions in the form of terraced and pronged buildings are developed ("a change in the situation") through the design experiments, the specific plot dimensions are painfully experienced and the pine

---

49 Ammon 2015: 190.
50 See Einstein 1916, 1973, Mach 1906.
51 See Bolzano 1837, Faste and Faste 2012.
52 Schön 1983: 68.

forest is discovered and appreciated ("a new understanding of the phenomenon"). Consequently, the world is not first analyzed and then designed through the practical activity of design but is instead experimentally both changed and examined in one go by design. Thus, according to Schön, a design does not respond to the special needs of a context, but instead also clarifies it and to a certain extent explains it.[53] When designing, there is thus no clear differentiation between the definition of a problem and its solution; problem definition and problem solution are two sides of the same coin. Their relationship is reciprocal.[54] In this metaphor, design can be understood as the coin possessing both a changing and an examining side: change and knowledge gain, creation and reflection, art and science; this dual function is a central feature of design thought processes.[55] As stated by architecture theoretician Gerd de Bruyn, design produces the synthesis of scientific and artistic work and also reflects upon this product.[56] Design is thus not only synthesis but, to a certain extent, also the producer and reflection of itself.

To answer the question whether design is analysis or synthesis we can sum up by saying: Since reality is not first analyzed by practical activity and then subsequently synthesized, but is instead experimentally both changed and examined at the same time in the design process, analytical and synthetic aspects of the act of designing can be differentiated in retrospect, but the act of designing itself is not separated into analysis and synthesis and methodically subdivided.[57] Instead, one must approach design with a concept of reciprocal changing and examination. In the following, we will first touch on the core qualities of the changing dimension to then illuminate the examining dimension of design in greater depth.

Design both finds and invents potential and resources

Reality is changed, at least conceptually, in the design process. To this end, alternative possibilities are presented for an existing situation. These alternatives point out possible potential. Accordingly, potential is the product of the changing dimension of the

---

53 Kühn 2009: 170.
54 Alexander 1964: 91.
55 See Spencer-Brown 1969.
56 De Bruyn 2008: 21.
57 The dual concept of "analysis/synthesis" is far too removed from the inner logic of design for this purpose. This procedure would tend to blur design rather than clarify it.

design, and design is a tool for making potential visible. In order to represent this, we look once again to the example of the hotel design: The slope on the ocean side serves here as the existing situation. It is read and interpreted. The ocean view is intuitively assigned potential before designing is commenced with. The first design attempt takes place subsequent to this. This represents the slab standing parallel with the coastline as an imagined future in which the potential of the ocean view is hypothetically activated. (Figure 1a) In the subsequent designs (Figures 1b–d), the relationship of the hotel rooms with the pine forest are recognized entirely incidentally as a further potential alongside the ocean view. The iterative design loops have thus also paid off in this respect. New potential was found through them.

The example shows the tightly interwoven relationship between design and potential: Potential is the ascribing of possibilities in specific networks of context and first appears when its elaboration is represented. Design is here the tool that makes this potential visible in that it represents alternative possibilities for an existing situation. The recognition and activation of potential is thus also dependent upon respective design-related, projective processes. In the process, existing potential is found, and new contexts of meaning are invented. In this light, the question arises whether potentials are pre-existent and can be found through designing, or whether potentials first arise through designing – and therefore have to be invented? The answer is ambiguous. The boundary between finding and inventing is fluid, as existing potential can only then be found when it emerges in a vision of the future, which must of course be invented.[58] Conversely, new potential can only then be invented when it arises, in the broadest sense, from the encountered reality.[59] Designing is thereby more than the application of certain materials and techniques or the leveraging of a certain amount of existing potential. It is the ability to think about future, not yet thought about ideas and to convert supposedly unconnected notions into coherent patterns of thought.[60] In the process, very specific potential can be crystallized to achieve a potential and desired change in a particular context. It can therefore be concluded that design simultaneously finds and invents potential.

58 See Rorty 2007.
59 Von Foerster 1993: 134–148.
60 See Kretz and Salewski 2014.

In the next stage, to translate this latent potential into a reliable resource, it must be possible to activate the discovered potential.[61] To leverage the potential of the ocean view and pine forest for future guests in the example of the hotel, the new constructions of meaning must be conveyed, strong investors of capital must be convinced, legally sound planning documents must be created, well-designed and economically viable working drawings must be drafted and capable craftsmen must be found and provided with plans. Once these criteria have been convincingly met, the approaches can finally be developed into an architectural strategy by identifying relevant potential and consolidating this into purpose-specific procedures.[62] The following can thus be claimed: When a design takes not only imaginary, but also strategic components of realization into consideration with regard to the design, it not only points out potential, but also transforms the bearers of potential into resources that can be mobilized. To this extent, a resource can be considered a leveragable source of potential. This is not a given but must instead first be found or invented and then proven. Design can thus be understood in the broadest sense as *the finding and inventing of resources*. At this transition point between potential and resource, the presumably harmless and playful creativity of design suddenly loses its innocence and takes on a proverbial creating aspect, in the sense of manufacturing or producing. Here if not before, the changing dimension of design assumes its societal, and thus political dimension.

However, how does this tie in with Schön's statement – namely that the design process can not only change an existing situation, and thus create potential and resources, but instead generate a new understanding of reality and achieve "a new understanding of the phenomenon"? The emergence of the pine forest in the hotel example is a first sign that design can throw up new perspectives on reality. This phenomenon will be explored in the next chapter.

---

61 See Feger 1985, Hoch 2007.
62 Healey 2009a: 452–453, Albrechts 2004: 751–752, see Ozbekhan 1969, Van den Broeck 2013.

2
Design as examination

As demonstrated in the last chapter, design is an action that simultaneously changes and tests reality. In a duet, the changing dimension and the examining dimension propel the design process. Appreciation of the two dimensions is, however, very unbalanced: While the changing dimension of design in each project is expressed visibly and is therefore described everywhere as the creative core of the designing activity, the examining dimension of design often remains invisible in contrast. Its property of promoting knowledge is difficult to comprehend. In numerous discussions with students, practicing architects, urban planners and research colleagues, it turned out that the examining dimension of design was usually only recognized indirectly. The cause for this seems to be that the design process is considered to be a sequential procedure. As already explained, the general assumption is that analysis and synthesis are two different sub-phases that are clearly differentiated from one another in terms of their processes. Design is summarily allocated to the latter phase and exclusively understood as synthesis as a result. The examining quality of design is suppressed by this broadly held, erroneous theoretical construct. However, this conclusion is short-sighted and far-reaching. Among other things, it means that purely empirical analyses are accepted as a means to knowledge, but that design is mostly viewed "only" as a personal idea or as an individual wish and is accordingly dismissed to the realm of unfounded speculation. In order to counter this, the focus will be shifted to the explanatory aspect within the design process which will be illuminated below. To this end, we explore how design can very well also serve as an analytical or protoempirical tool.

Design as a means to acquiring insight

Schön's "use/test-entity" mentioned above presumes that a "theory" or "leading idea" is not only used in every design operation, but that design is also an "experimental examination".[63] The experimental has two functions in this context. First, an examination takes place to determine whether the design

63 See Gedenryd 1998.

operation can even be carried out in the existing context or not. The design is tested on reality, so to speak. The point of view can, however, also be turned around, and reality is then tested on the design. This second experimental function examines whether reality can not only be changed by the design but can also be perceived as changed. With this change in perspective, an existing situation can be placed at the center of interest, and the design becomes the means for examining this encountered reality. Here, one finds the quintessence of Schön's statement that "[...] he carries out an experiment which serves to generate [...] a new understanding of the phenomenon."[64] The goal of design is in this case to provoke new insights. In order to illustrate the role of design as a means for examination in the service of a deeper understanding of reality, another simple example from the design process will be briefly presented: the transfer experiment. (Figure 4)

At the northern edge of Zurich, an urban planning project is to be realized which will urbanize a space containing several underused areas and, in the process, improve the spatial relationships with the immediate neighborhood. (Figure 4, top) As the guiding idea, the student design team would like to transfer the urban design features of the late 19th century *Gründerzeit* districts the students think very highly of to the outer district. The desired design is presented in the form of an aerial sketch. (Figure 4, bottom) The changing nature of this design attempt is obvious: a newly concentrated urban structure is to replace the residual areas representing the vision of the future strived for. However, a look at the draft sketch immediately awakens a sense of unease: the infrastructure barriers surrounding the area, which fragment the territory and divide it into relatively small compartments, make the idea of an expansive quarter with cohesive streets impossible. In addition, the contextual conditions cannot be improved upon as hoped with this design approach, and more than a third of all buildings would be completely unprotected from street noise.[65] Like an experiment, the design thus reveals a significant structural feature of the existing situation through its obvious failure: fragmentation due

64 Schön 1983: 68.
65 The perimeter pattern used in the transfer experiment was developed at a time when the physical continuity of cities was still for the most part present, with the exception of rivers and a few railway lines. Motorways did not cut through the cities of the 19th century. However, the urban topography in Zurich North is not contiguous; this is prevented by caesuras. Zurich North is also subjected to the noise of aircraft taking off and landing. Attempting to solve this issue with the perimeter pattern is therefore also unsuitable.

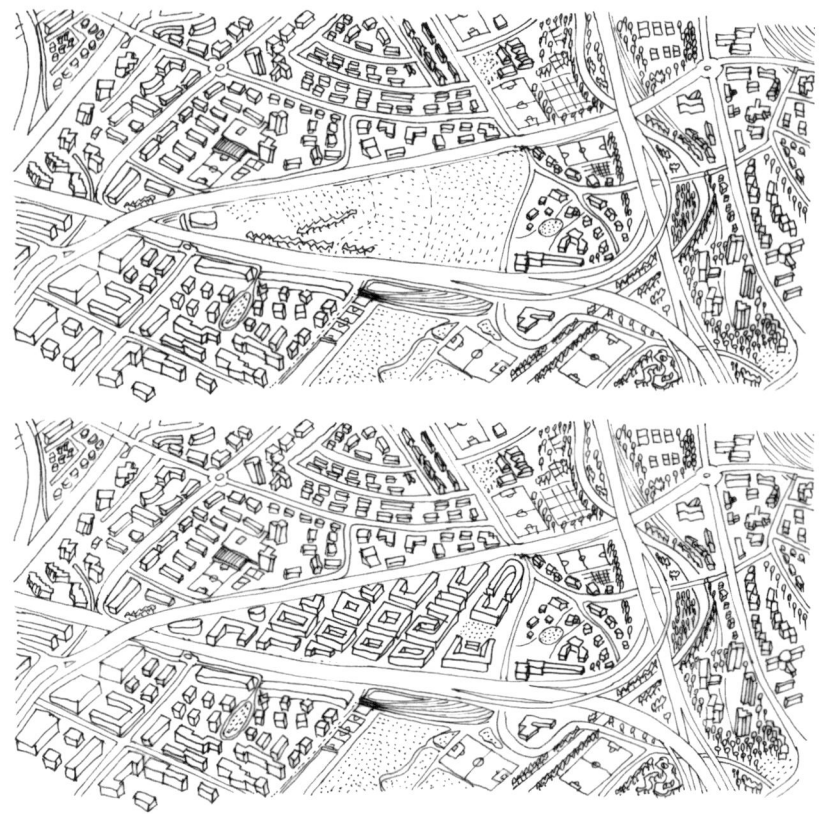

Figure 4.
The transfer experiment

to heavy-duty infrastructure. The consequence of this design experiment is a changed understanding of the situation and an altered definition of the problem. The focus of interest is now shifted to the edges and boundaries of the area burdened by infrastructure. In the subsequent design process, this changed problem definition will very likely also lead to an altered solution, thus to a reformulation of the guiding urban planning idea and of the suggested project. The experiment triggers an entire cascade of new perceptions, insights, ideas and concepts.

A thesis by Swiss architect Marcel Meili can help us pursue this view of design as an experiment even further. Meili credits design with the potential to expand the "conceptual space and sphere of action [...] as the gentle application of force to reality extending to the pain threshold". So that on the one hand "conceptual space and sphere of action" are broadened through design while the "pain threshold" of "reality", on the other, becomes perceptible or visible.[66] This allows the conclusion that Schön's "new understanding of the phenomenon" can be achieved when the design sounds out the possible "sphere of action" and its conditions extending to its "pain threshold". In the example of the periphery of Zurich, it is the attempt to inscribe properties of the city center into the fragmented urban landscape which, through its failure, makes the "pain thresholds" visible in the form of severing infrastructures. The possible "sphere of action" is also changed by the experiment because after the experiment the focus of interest is no longer on the expansion of the perimeter structure to residual areas, but instead on the designing of the peripheries and boundaries, and thus on the redefining of the new "conceptual space and sphere of action". This "conceptual space and sphere of action" is the framework for consideration, so to speak, which is first altered by the experimental design and subsequently examined with additional drafts.[67] The most important insight to retain here is that the experience of the "pain threshold of reality" can be provoked through design, and that, as a consequence of this, both the assessment of the existing reality and the conceptual space and sphere of action are changed. We have now arrived at the essence of Schön's thesis. This says that the design operations possess an examining dimension because specific properties of the existing situation can be explored and revealed when designing through targeted interventions. In the example of the periphery of Zurich, the intervention corresponds with the projected perimeter structure, which allows the specific structural characteristic of the fragmented urban landscape to become apparent. It can thus be determined that designing not only means the testing of an operation on reality, but also that reality is examined with this operation. Design thereby becomes an investigative means to acquiring new insights.

66 Meili 2011.
67 See Schön and Rein 1994.

Problem areas of design

After demonstrating that design can be used as the means for examining reality, we should try to determine which realities a design-based examination of this kind might call for. Many problems of the world are much easier to understand, meaning design methods need not even be applied at all for their examination.[68] Mathematician and physicist Horst Rittel already mentioned in the design as a process section above, also differentiates "wicked problems" from comparatively simply structured ones.[69] The former are vexing, complex, unclear and contrary.[70] According to Rittel, in their complexity, vagueness and contradiction, they are neither easily surmountable nor completely comprehensible. They cannot be uniformly processed or even objectified in methodological terms.[71] Tasks in architecture and urban planning are such vexing problems. They mostly manifest themselves as a bundle of ambiguous, individual problems from different disciplines existing in obvious contradiction with one another,[72] and they recognize no clearly correct or false solution but can instead only be solved for better or worse.[73] Their respective uniqueness, contingency, openness, cultural conditionality, interdisciplinary complexity, emergent nature and both ethical and aesthetic disputability makes them "wicked problems" par excellence.

In the case of "wicked problems", the object of examination is so dynamic and complex that purely empirical analyses are completely inadequate. While these can illuminate individual aspects, they cannot comprehend the problems as a whole.[74] The examining potential of design reveals itself in this context: in contrast with analytical procedures, design does not attempt to split complex problems into as many simple and distinct sub-problems as possible. Entirely on the contrary: holistic intervention and manipulation is integral to design. It is precisely these properties that make design thought processes the appropriate means for tackling "wicked problems" because, in keeping with their complex and emergent nature, these cannot simply be split into their individual parts. Thanks to its portending,

---

68 See Polya 1945.
69 Rittel 1992: 75.
70 See Simon 1973, Lyotard 1983: 9–16.
71 See Protzen and Harris 2010.
72 Rittel 1992: 75, see Venturi [1966] 2003: 25.
73 See Cross 2006.
74 See Dörner 1974, 2001, Schönwandt 1986, Vester 1999, Lawson 1980, 1994, 2004.

interpretive and especially interventionist and transforming nature, design is a suitable means for examining the "spheres of action", limits and conditions of "wicked problems" as a whole, without having to understand all individual elements in detail in the confusing problem areas.[75]

However, not all design operations are suited *a priori* to promoting a better understanding of "wicked problems". Only those designs that use explanation, interpretation and manipulation – not only as ends in themselves but also as the experimental means for the examination of the existing reality – have the potential to advance knowledge.[76] The example of the Zurich periphery once again serves to illustrate this: if the design sketch with the *Gründerzeit* building structure had been used as pure vision, the presence of the infrastructure corridors surrounding it would not have been worthy of further notice. The belief in the projective means to an end would have suppressed the emergence of the problem. As a critical experiment, however, the sketch enables the knowledge that the compartmentalization of the urban landscape is the central design problem, and not the area to be built upon. The comprehension of reality newly won through the design can be viewed as an experiential surplus of the design action. This experiential surplus has two qualities. First, it initiates, in the protoanalytical sense, further examinations as theses or questions. Secondly, these new theses and questions themselves stimulate design and lead to new ideas and approaches to solutions. On this topic, Meili notes the following:

> *The speculative, tentative and vague character of theses, the temporary unverifiability of programmatic intentions or theoretical claims [...] is not a weakness, but instead a specific characteristic of design thought processes. [...] It creates room to maneuver for the project.*[77]

Design-related problems are thus not only vexing and complex but are in fact for this reason also inexhaustible sources for fathoming the realm of possibility of various solutions and for innovation.[78]

75 See Forester 1989: 119–133.
76 See Christensen 1985, Eisinger 2008, Secchi and Vigano 2009.
77 Meili 2006.
78 See Salewski 2014.

Design as qualitative-heuristic experimentation

According to the physician and naturalist Galen, open, vexing and principally unsolvable problems require a third form in addition to the two more familiar forms of examination, empiricism and logic. This third form is the "comprehension" that emerges "from the world of appearances" and "out of the darkness" and which leads to a "method or to ordered knowledge".[79] This form of knowledge creation primarily involves an open-ended procedure.[80] The large number of empirically observable individual aspects should, according to Galen, thus solidify into comprehensible theses and representations through ordering, relationalization and systematization. In the process, it must be remembered that these theses and representations are initially completely unknown and invisible and only assume contours gradually. This is thus a process of understanding that occurs equally through discovery and invention, involving qualitative analysis *and* creation.[81] The contrast of this form of experimental "groping" with a laboratory experiment, which tests consistent hypotheses with the exclusion of all unknowns, becomes clear here: design may also be a structuring, yet genuinely open process of discovery. Donald Schön describes this as follows:

When planners [...] convert an uncertain situation into a solvable problem, they construct [...] not only the means to be deployed but the ends-in-view to be achieved. In such problem-setting, ends and means are reciprocally determined.[82]

Expanding on this, Schön writes:

[...] and often, in the unstable world of practice, where methods and theories developed in one context are unsuited to another, practitioners function as researchers, inventing the techniques and models appropriate to the situation at hand.[83]

This characteristic has been aptly named "structuring discovery"[84] by Sebastian Klüsener, and thus anchors the design, created as an examination, in qualitative heuristics. Heuristics occupies itself with the development and use of processes of

79 Galen [approx. 200 AD] 1528: 4r/v.
80 See Oechslin 2012b: 585.
81 Schleiermacher [1814] 1988: 5, Von Foerster 1993: 134–148, see Ungers 1982: 7–9.
82 Schön 1985: 15.
83 Ibid: 15.
84 Klüsener 1998: 1.

discovery involving open, not easily definable and complex problems.[85] Conspicuous here is that no exact processes can be defined for this. The peculiarities of "wicked problems" can be manifestly accessed neither with numbers nor with measurements, nor with previously designed processes for the generation of form.[86] Their already mentioned properties of openness, contingency, complexity and contextuality make the use of codes or regularities impossible. Entirely to the contrary: both the sociologist, Gerhard Kleining, and the scientific theoretician, Paul Feierabend, emphasize that the constant adaptation of methods to the object to be examined, as Schön also determined for design, is a fundamental strategy for action in heuristics.[87] The urban planner and theoretician, Manuel de Solà-Morales, supports this insight when he polemically claims that a deep understanding of the laws of transformation of cities requires much more than the sterile certitude of methods of analysis.[88] Accordingly, the manifold and differing observations and practical experiences should not be limited unnecessarily, but should instead be gradually described, condensed and made comprehensible for others. Which brings us back to what Galen referred to as "comprehension".

In his pioneering essay *Umriss zu einer Methodologie qualitativer Sozialforschung* [Outline for a Methodology of Qualitative Social Research], Kleining describes that findings in heuristic processes are not first formulated abstractly and then tested concretely, but can instead only be condensed gradually and through many iterative experiments.[89] Typical processes of qualitative heuristics are conjectures, theses, analogies and thought experiments.[90] They all serve the discovery of new knowledge, without attempting to establish its complete truth, because this knowledge exists only temporarily in a relationship with that knowledge yet to be found.[91] Viewed from this perspective, design can be understood as an experimentally organized questioning of the reality to be examined, which provides the designer with possible, but not with fixed answers. In *Die Macht des Erscheinens* [The Power of Manifestation], the aesthetician, Martin Seel, emphasizes that thought experiments in particular

85   See Hartkopf et al. 1987.
86   List 2009: 327.
87   Kleining [1986] 1994: 162, see Feierabend 1976.
88   Solà-Morales 1992: 197.
89   Kleining [1982] 1994: 12–46.
90   See Kühne 2005, Moravánszky 2015.
91   See Latour 2007: 359.

are ultimately aimed at constituting possible worlds.[92] In his opinion, it is less about determining whether something is true or false, but instead whether it is possible or necessary. In keeping with this, design is a seeking and provocative dialogue with reality. In the process, experimental thinking is a suitable means for crystallizing the structural properties, limits and conditions of existing reality, especially in the context of failure.[93] The central role that failure plays for new knowledge is also documented by the two examples presented. Both with the hotel design and with the transfer experiment in the north of Zurich, it is precisely the failed designs that have allowed the existing basic conditions and structural limits to surface. Plot geometry, pine forest and the infrastructure dominance are cognitive products of failure. In this context, it should be added that the failure of design experiments should not be perceived as negative, but instead as an important means to knowledge, which leads to new Eureka! moments.

Looking back at Schön's thesis, "He carries out an experiment which serves to generate both a new understanding of the phenomenon and a change in the situation", the "experiment" can now be defined more precisely as a design in the sense of a qualitative-heuristic (thought) experiment.[94]

The rationalization of the existing

In order to understand design as a more general cognitive operation, it should be noted that the form of dealing with reality developed by Schön and examined further in this work spans an interdisciplinary range extending well beyond the mentioned natural and social sciences. It is not difficult, for example, to also recognize a close relationship with realist art, which, according to art historian Klaus Herding, has "not only an informing influence [...] on the respective reality [...] but is also transformative and enlightening".[95] According to cultural philosopher Ernst Cassirer, there is – as an extension to the concept of knowledge – an "experiencing" ("Erleben" or living through),[96] which provides the actual foundation for our reference to the world,

92 Seel 2007: 38.
93 Kleining [1986] 1994: 173–176, Heidegger [1927] 2001: 73.
94 Because design usually has to do with future states, many design experiments are of a speculative nature. Nonetheless, designs can also be real experiments, in that they are executed. An architectural or urban planning project can thus be understood as a real experiment with its design.
95 Herding, in Pfisterer 2011: 372.
96 Cassirer [1925] 1994: II 187.

both within and outside of the strict sciences: "It is not just observation but action that forms the epicenter from which the mental organization of reality starts for human beings".[97] This "experiencing" expresses itself in language, as well as in myths, religion, art or architecture.[98] Design is in this context a trial action, a "conceptual experience", so to speak, with which the world is experimentally changed and can thus also be better understood. In the context of the architectural and urban planning discipline, reference should be made to the famous research project by Oswald Mathias Ungers and his pupils, *Berlin, ein grünes Archipel: Die Stadt in der Stadt*[99] [Berlin, a green archipelago: the city within the city], Rem Koolhaas' *Delirious New York*[100], and the urban study of Robert Venturi, Denise Scott Brown and Steven Izenour, *Learning from Las Vegas*.[101] All authors explicitly utilize urban planning design projects or other forms of speculative thinking to experience the respective reality in design. (Figure 5) Due to an absence of appropriate overarching urban theories, all three studies thereby avoid general concepts concerning the cities they examine. Very much on the contrary: the respective, specific realities are accepted, precisely understood, experimentally manipulated and only then are they gradually distilled into manifestos of themselves. In order to crystallize these manifestos from the cities, they are "experienced" by the authors through, amongst other methods, the qualitative-heuristic approach of experimental design.[102] Discoveries originate from competition projects, field studies and hypothetical drafts, which are then subjected to a speculative logic, expressed in publications as theses and represented as models. Koolhaas describes this design process as a "retroactive theorization",[103] where what has been experienced, learned and designed is verbalized, not as a certainty, but instead as a claim in the sense of a possible but not certain description of reality. The existing is thus tentatively subjected to a speculative logic. In *Delirious New York*, Koolhaas exemplifies this by presenting the urbanization of Manhattan as a delirious process of a modernist-capitalist logic that resulted in a radical threefold separation from its inner rationality: The separation of infrastructure and land,

97 Ibid
98 See Blumenberg 2006.
99 Ungers et al. [1977] 2013.
100 Koolhaas 1978.
101 Venturi, Scott Brown and Izenour 1977.
102 See Simpson 2008.
103 See Koolhaas 1978, Bideau 2011: 23.

the separation of form and content and, since the introduction of the elevator, the vertical separation of various uses per story in the skyscrapers. (Figure 5, bottom right) Koolhaas thus conceptualizes and portrays Manhattan in an exemplary manner as the product of an endless chain of repetitions of these three separations.[104]

According to Venturi, Scott Brown and Izenour, in Las Vegas the logic of the automobile has so fundamentally altered the attention economy of human beings that Las Vegas has now been built in keeping with the principles of automotive mobility.[105] (Figure 5, top left) Building on this, the authors describe Las Vegas retroactively as a product of this logic. In order to gain a sensual and intellectual access to this phenomenon, Venturi, Scott Brown and Izenour have subjected themselves to this specific reality of Las Vegas. They photographically recorded the Strip of Las Vegas through the windshield, learned from this experience, and then mapped and internalized the principles of this city, thus speculatively designing the logic inherent in the city. (Figure 5, top right) The programmatic book title, *Learning from Las Vegas*, bears witness to this methodological self-conception, which focuses on the specific particularities of the examined city and its internalization.[106]

Although Venturi, Scott Brown and Izenour and Koolhaas deal with different themes of contemporary urbanization and make recourse to various cultural roots, they share the method of structuring discovery by way of speculative logic.[107] Conscious of this methodological approach, and looking back at his own speculative study, *Berlin, ein grünes Archipel: Die Stadt in der Stadt*[108], Ungers explicitly named the slow process of the structuring discovery of an initially still unknown phenomenon as "the rationalization of the existing".[109] This is probably the most concise formula for the form of knowledge referred to as "comprehension" called for by Galen, which "originates from the world of appearances" and "from the darkness", and "gradually leads to method and to ordered knowledge". In his biography of Ungers, Jasper Cepl describes this process as an expressive act of will, which creates the conscious out of the unconsciously

---

104 As a methodological point, it should be mentioned here that the speculative logic of the monetary capital investment, which, according to Koolhaas, created Manhattan, is reflected in the speculative logic of the designing method of Koolhaas. In this case, the method has even adapted to the specific particularities of the object examined, and this as an analogy.
105 Venturi, Scott Brown and Izenour 1977.
106 Ibid, see Stierli 2010.
107 While in *Learning from Las Vegas*, for example, the relationship of image and reality is taken up as a theme and builds on a background of communications theory and anthropology, *Delirious New York* has its roots in a psychoanalytical tradition and thereby thematizes the retroactive historiography, the manifest irony and, in the process, represents the city as the product of regulatory processes based on principles of the market economy and on the logistical reduction of complexity.

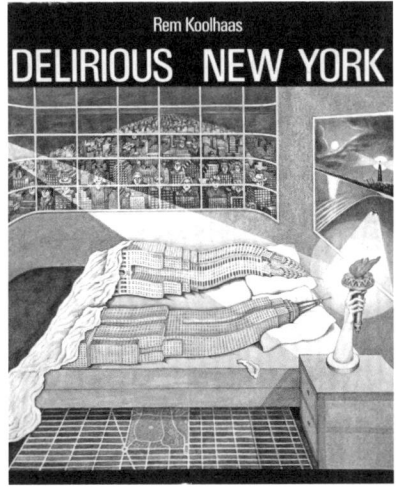

Figure 5.
Rationalizations of the existing
(Venturi, Scott Brown and Izenour 1977, Koolhaas 1978)

108 In this work Ungers describes Berlin as being subject to the logic of the shrinking city. This ratio leads inevitably to a new wilderness in the city center and at the same time forces the retreat of the urban into highly selective city fragments. Among other things, *Berlin, ein grünes Archipel: Die Stadt in der Stadt* explores the changing shape of the city, its radical secularization and the role of monuments, including their profanization.

109 Ungers, Koolhaas and Obrist 2006: 6-11, see Ungers [1981] 2011.

existing.[110] Ungers refers to the role of this awareness process as "something that registers reality through sensual experience and imagination".[111] It is a creative process, because it achieves a higher degree of order than the simple methods of measuring, testing and checking. Ungers thereby differentiates between three basic levels on which phenomena can be comprehended:[112]

1. The discovery of pure facts
2. The psychological impression or the psychological reception inside us
3. The imaginative discovery and reconstruction of phenomena, in order to conceptualize them

According to Ungers, designing is primarily the latter: "It is always a fundamental process of the conceptualization of an independent, diverse and therefore varied reality through the use of ideas, imaginations, metaphors, analogies, models, signs, symbols and allegories".[113] These tools are imaginative structures of meaning that pervade all human understanding and thought. They not only depict a prescribed reality, but instead actively reconstruct reality from an implicitly available repertoire that has its roots in what has been experienced and lived.[114] In keeping with this, the sculptor, graphic artist and designer, Otto Aicher, describes design as an active construction of reality, which grows out of the intellectual ordering and clarification of contexts, from the defining of dependencies and from the creation of weights and relevancies.[115] This presumes a special ability in the mind of the designer to see and fix analogies, contexts and fields of reference. Here too, this involves a description of an "imaginative discovery and [...] reconstruction of the phenomena" and its relationships "in order to conceptualize them".[116]

To summarize, it should be kept in mind that design can lead to a deep understanding of the specific, existing situation, in that the existing is transformatively examined, imaginatively discovered and intellectually reconstructed, and a qualitative statement with regard to reality is made in the form of a speculative logic.[117] This rationalization of the existing can thus also

110 Cepl 2007: 362, see Halbwachs [1939] 1950.
111 Ungers 1982: 8.
112 Ibid
113 Ibid: 9.
114 List 2009: 323.
115 Aicher 1991: 192.
116 Ungers 1982: 8.
117 See Simpson 2008.

be understood as a claim, or as "informed guessing"[118], and thus be either empirically further examined and tested or also serve as a new stimulus for the subsequent design process.

For purposes of illustration, the rationalization of the existing will be represented using the example of the urban periphery: (Figure 4) As with the aforementioned examples in Las Vegas and Manhattan, there is not yet an explanation or rule in the existing storehouse of knowledge that could deal with the example of Zurich's northern urban periphery. Classic and proven urban theories are either obsolete or not locally specific enough for the phenomenon in Zurich North. And because no appropriate type of explanation can be found by the students, a new one must be found in a mental process.[119] This is where the design experiment comes in: while unable to improve the existing situation by filling it with an urban texture of the *Gründerzeit*, the experiment allows us to examine the situation all the more critically. Due to the failure of this attempt, the design team becomes aware of the compartmentalization of the urban landscape. First only as a vague observation, as a diffuse description of the properties of the "world of phenomena", thus of "reality". With repeated observation and after mature consideration, the students can propose a thesis: the urban landscape follows a logic of fragmentation. This speculatively established logic is now tested by various means and examined further. In the process, it becomes clear that fragmentation not only affects the physical and ecological spaces in the presented example (through mobility infrastructures) but, increasingly, also the economic value creation potential (through the varying accessibility of the individual fragments) and the social milieus (through the absence of permeability between the fragments). Similar areas are then also examined, and the phenomenon of fragmentation is also found here. Supported by further observations, the thesis can now be condensed as a model and theoretically elaborated: the "infrastructure dominance in the contemporary city" is postulated. The fragmentation is thus no longer comprehended as a phenomenon of the examined territory at the periphery of Zurich, but instead in the sense of

[118] Peirce 1958: 7.219.
[119] See Reichertz 1999.

a logic of fragmentation as a fundamental process of urbanization of the city landscape. This emphasis is a "rationalization of the existing".

However, what does such an abstraction contribute to a "hypothetical speculation"?[120] What is the effect of such "rationalizations of the existing", in the sense of abstracted concepts, on concrete situations? According to the philosopher and educator, John Dewey, abstract concepts have an instrumental value, because they not only transcend concrete situations, but also open up new spheres of action.[121] The abstraction thus has a dual function here: it is at the same time design knowledge and design thesis. In the example of the Zurich periphery, by collecting social statistics on residents and people working in the area, by researching land prices and creating topological plans mapping bridges and tunnels, the developed logic of fragmentation can on the one hand be more precisely examined in terms of knowledge arising from design in subsequent analyses. On the other hand, as a thesis for design, this abstraction can also become the thematic starting point for further design experiments – for example, for affirmative, critical or opposing designs. The multitude of design approaches potentially stimulated by this thesis of fragmentation logic represented in the example is left to the reader's imagination. The key insight here is that design can lead to a deep understanding of the specific situation by experimentally examining and speculatively rationalizing the existing, thereby providing a qualitative statement on reality. As demonstrated in this chapter, the statements also find their way into the knowledge discourse, not as general rules or methodological schemata, but instead probably ideally in the form of commented design experiments, specific theses, sample collections and operational prototypes.

Abduction

The "rationalization of the existing" presented in the last section refers in a scientific theory context to the term of "abduction" which American mathematician, philosopher, logician,

---

120 Ungers [1981] 2011: 10.
121 Dewey [1938] 1997, see Kolb 1984: 9–10.

semiotician and decisive thinker of pragmatism Charles Sanders Peirce introduced to the scientific debate.[122] Similar to speculative logic, abduction describes a process in which an explanatory thesis is formulated. Peirce defines abduction as a hypothetical conclusion, aimed at a regularity, starting from the individual. It is applied when no suitable explanation for the understanding of a phenomenon can be found in the existing repository of knowledge. Abductive logic stands in opposition to the two other logical conclusions, deduction and induction. While deduction states that something must be, and induction points out that something is actually effective, abduction merely points out that something can be.[123] The abductive conclusion thus attempts to develop a possible explanation from something unknown, which contrasts with induction, for example, that reaches conclusions on similar cases on the basis of known cases.

Something unexpected or inexplicable stands at the start of abduction; something that cannot be classified into that already known and which triggers doubt in the validity of one's own ideas. Because no suitable explanation is at the ready, "a new one must be invented or found [...] in a mental process".[124] This "mental process" guides the inexplicable to a new logic. It is not dissimilar to Galen's "comprehension" described in the last chapter and "emerges from the world of appearances and out of the darkness, and leads to method or to knowledge with an open end".[125] This new logic is initially speculative, for Galen, as well as for Ungers and Peirce. It is not assured. The product of an abductive process is thus also a thesis, a claim. In the process, conclusions are reached relating to general principles or backgrounds that could explain observed data. An abductive conclusion can thus also be disproven with evidence.

According to Peirce, the formation of such a thesis is a creative conclusion, a conceptual leap that, like lightning, brings a new idea into the world and brings together things in such a way as one might think they could only impossibly be related to one another. Similar to the Eureka! moment described in Chapter 1, which was thematized by Einstein and Mach,[126] the philosopher Cornelius Delaney describes this act, referring back to Peirce,

---

122 Peirce 1958: 5.171.
123 Ibid
124 Reichertz 1999: 53.
125 Galen [approx. 200 AD] 1528: 4r/v.
126 See Einstein 1916, Mach 1906.

as a "discovery moment" that is "a matter of the creative imagination of some people".[127] According to this, abductive conclusions also differ from inductive conclusions due to the creative process with which they are achieved, and through the discovery of new contexts.[128] This also explains why Peirce understands abduction as a process that differs from deduction and induction in that it expands knowledge. Peirce legitimizes this as follows:

All the ideas of science come to it by the way of abduction. Abduction consists in studying facts and devising a theory to explain them. Its only justification is that if we ever do understand things at all, it must be in that way.[129]

According to German sociologist and communications scientist Jo Reichertz, "abductions occur", they cannot be intentionally forced, and they "do not occur when one conscientiously follows an operationalized program of processes".[130] This corresponds to the view held by Kleining who claims in the context of the qualitative-heuristic experiment that no exact processes can be defined.[131] However, how can one provoke these "incidents" when they can neither be generated nor explained with rational processes? According to Peirce, there are two principal behaviors and provisions that provoke abductive moments or prepare the mind in such a way that abductive lightning can strike at all. The first maxim for action states that one should enter into situations that link real doubt, fear or great pressure to act with the will to learn:

No matter how erroneous your ideas of the method may be at first, you will be forced at length to correct them so long as your activity is moved by [...] sincere desire. [...] In order to demonstrate that this is so, it is necessary to note what is essentially involved in the Will to Learn. The first thing that the Will to Learn supposes is a dissatisfaction with one's present state of opinion.[132]

Doubt thereby provides the foundation for abandoning existing certainties; the will to learn and curiosity allow for the possibility to seriously consider new perspectives and explanatory approaches; and the high degree of pressure to act creates

---
127 Delaney 1993: 15.
128 Stangl 2018.
129 Peirce [1903] 1997: 218.
130 Reichertz 1999: 54.
131 Kleining [1986] 1994: 162.
132 Peirce [1898] 1929: 170–171.

emergency situations in which one must take action, and in which new theses and speculative logics are forced, so to speak. In these emergency situations, doubt, the will to learn and the pressure to act unite, thus often resulting, Peirce believes, in abductive lightning.[133]

The second maxim for action is of an opposing nature. It states that one should allow the mind to wander without a goal. Peirce calls this unreflecting strolling "musement" – daydreaming:[134]

Enter your skiff of musement, push off into the lake of thought, and leave the breath of heaven to swell your sail. With your eyes open, awake to what is about or within you, and open conversation with yourself: for such is all meditation! It is, however, not a conversation in words alone, but is illustrated, like a lecture, with diagrams and with experience.[135]

This second quote is very reminiscent of Bruno Taut's description featured at the beginning of the book, which presents design as a shift from "thinking" to "feeling". A condition is invoked here where "consciously working reason, familiar with logical rules, is outmaneuvered".[136] This is also the case with both of Peirce's maxims for action. In the first maxim, the emergency situation, reason is given no time to occupy itself with the solution to its problem. Which is why the instinct to guess assumes responsibility for this task. With the second maxim, by daydreaming, logical judgement is deactivated in favor of a wandering of thoughts not urgently calling for action.[137]

The specific abduction form of design

Design plays two roles in this abductive process. (Figure 6) The first role describes design as a creativity technique that in a sense undermines the rational understanding of order, because it experimentally allows new perceptions to arise.[138] This explains those famous lost-in-thought, "daydreamer" scribblings of architects in their sketchbooks. As (thought) experiments, designs serve the purpose of an irritation of perception, and thus as stimuli for new discoveries. (Figure 6, part A) These new

133 Ibid: 271.
134 Reichertz 1999: 56.
135 Peirce 1958: 6.461.
136 Reichertz 1999: 57.
137 Ibid
138 See Lenk 2000.

discoveries, which are experimentally provoked, change the image of reality that the designer or team had prior to designing. (Figure 6, part B) Both images – the one prior to the discovery and the other subsequent to it – generate a difference through their dissimilarity. In a best-case scenario, this difference generates something like an "aha" effect, and the newly acquired understanding of reality enters consciousness. Up to this point, design is not yet abductive, but instead protoabductive, because it initially "only" generates the new perceptions and data, but no conclusions are reached yet. (Figure 6, parts A and B) The abduction that subsequently follows is accordingly prepared by the protoabductive role of the design; the mind is receptive to the abductive flash of lightning.

This flash of inspiration describes the second role of design as an abductive step *per se*. Here, design becomes speculation, because it attempts to create a possible logic and formulate this as a thesis. (Figure 6, part C) In order to emphasize this, the description of Ungers should be remembered, which states that design not only experimentally changes reality, but also imaginatively discovers and reconstructs phenomena in order to conceptualize them. According to Ungers, design is a process of the conceptualization of any kind of reality using ideas, imaginations, metaphors, analogies, models, signs, symbols and allegories.[139]

While the first protoabductive role of design originates from "musement", from daydreaming, the second, abductive role is born more out of the emergency situation, in which a possible rationalization is almost forced. This especially applies when those outside the design team need explanations why something has been done or what the design hopes to achieve. In these situations, rationalization "from outside" is called for. This leads to a pressure moment where the long period of "musement" must be compiled in a highly condensed form as logic for it to be communicated at all. The result is a thesis, a speculative logic of reality.

---

139 Ungers 1982: 9.

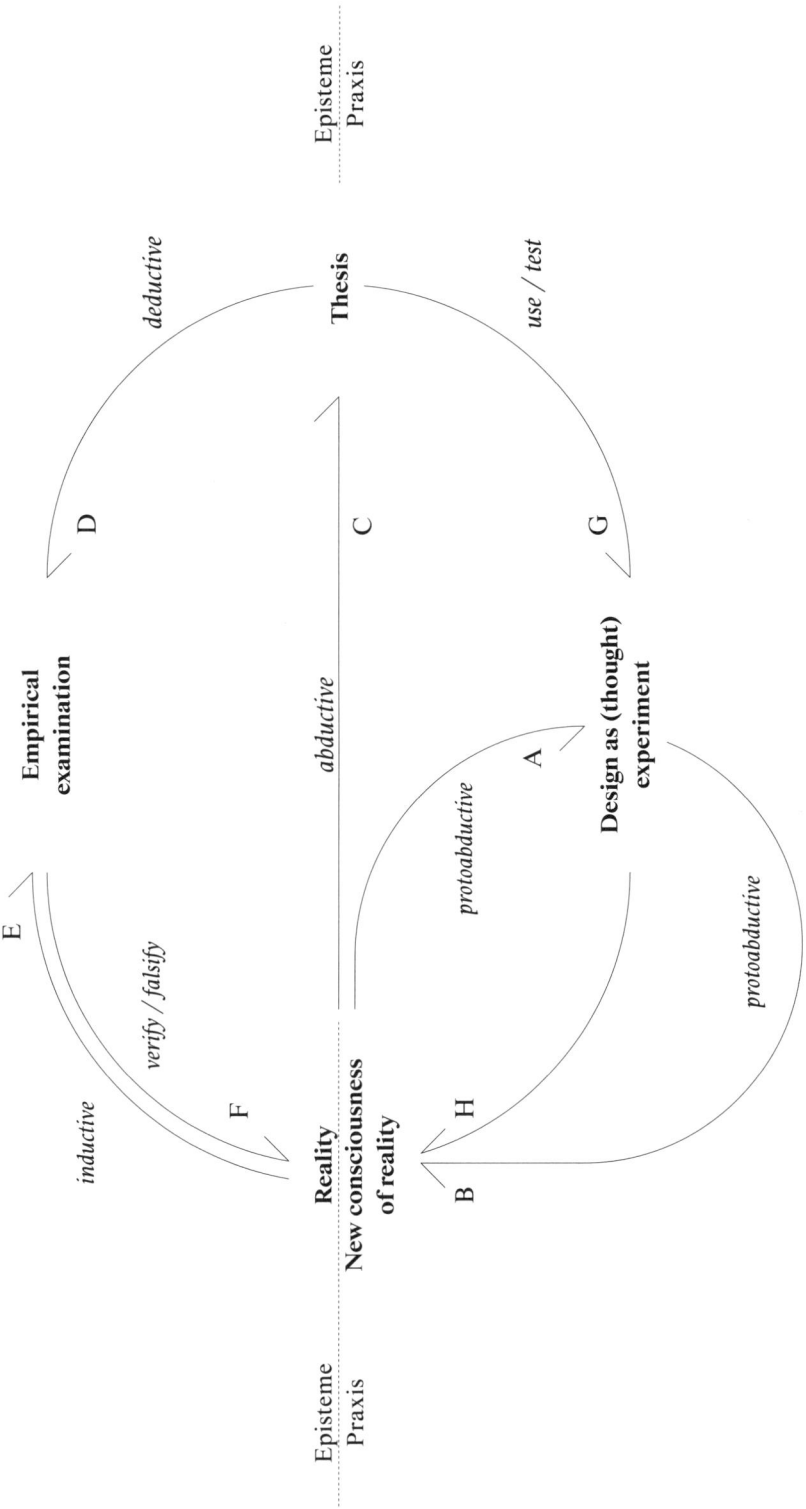

Figure 6.
*The specific abduction form of design and
its embedding in the double loop of knowledge creation*

Once speculative logic of this kind regarding reality has been formulated, as took place in the example of Zurich North with the claim of a "logic of fragmentation", the abductive step is initially completed. Formulated as a thesis, it triggers two processes: the critical checking and the practical application of this thesis. While the critical checking is of a scientific nature, the practical application of the thesis stimulates the design. Both processes will be briefly presented below.

The first process following abduction is the critical check. This takes place with Peirce's triadic cognitive logic, which consists of abduction, deduction and induction.[140] The abductively acquired thesis is the first level of the triad. The second step is deduction, where forecasts are derived from the thesis as a kind of conclusion. (Figure 6, part D) This is followed by the third step, induction. Individual cases are gathered in the process in order to verify the presuppositions. (Figure 6, part E) In the simplest case, the inductive conclusions of the individual cases agree with the deductively derived conclusions of the original thesis. The thesis is thus transported into a newly checked "rule"; something new has been recognized. (Figure 6, part F) However, if the inductively determined "rule" does not agree with the initial thesis, the process must be commenced again with a changed thesis.[141] Irrespective of whether something new is recognized or not, this process in any case also creates a changed understanding of reality.

In the example in Zurich North, the path from the protoabductive role of design through the abductive conclusion to the cognitive triad can be described as follows: through its failure, the design experiment with the perimeter structure creates not only doubt with regard to the known approach to a solution, but especially also with respect to the nature of reality. (Figure 6, part A) The experiment reveals the relevance of the infrastructure corridors and creates a new perspective on reality. (Figure 6, part B) These infrastructure corridors are the metaphorical starting gun for a cognitive expedition into the unknown. So much for the protoabductive step. From this, a thesis is now speculatively formed in the abductive step: Zurich North follows

140 As already described, the abductive logic exists in opposition to the two other logical conclusions. While deduction states that something must be, and induction points out that something is actually effective, abduction merely points out that something can be (Peirce 1958: 5.171). Abduction attempts to apprehend the origination of theses, in contrast with, for example, induction, where conclusions are reached for similar cases on the basis of known cases.

141 See Gleiter 2017: 99.

the logic of fragmentation. (Figure 6, part C) One can now deductively infer from this claim, which Peirce paraphrased as a "guess", in the sense of inferences based on forecasts, the following: if Zurich North is characterized by a comprehensive logic of fragmentation, then all spatial situations as of a certain size must principally be fragmented in Zurich North to the extent possible. (Figure 6, part D) This inference can now be inductively checked, thus leading from many individual cases to the general. The thesis is in fact supported by the individual cases. No district can be found in Zurich North that has not been characterized by the logic of fragmentation. (Figure 6, part E) The thesis is thus proven. (Figure 6, part F)

However, why is a critical check even necessary at all? Reichertz addresses this question by tracing the unreliability of abductive conclusions. Because, according to Reichertz, the abductive flash is accompanied by an unpleasant feeling that is more convincing than any probability calculation, but is unfortunately all too frequently wrong.[142] Peirce believe this is because abductions result from processes that cannot be rationally argued and criticized.

Abduction is that kind of operation which suggests a statement in no wise contained in the data from which it sets out. There is a more familiar name for it than abduction; for it is neither more nor less than guessing.[143]

An empirical follow-up check is unavoidable for this reason. In addition to the critical check, the second process, which is triggered by the abduction, encompasses the practical application of the thesis in design. The concept, propagated by Schön, of design as the simultaneous "use and testing" of a "guiding idea" or of a "thesis" once again comes into play. (Figure 6, part G) The thesis is namely not only protoempirical, but also stimulates design. It thus serves not just the purpose of being able to describe reality, but also of finding a normative guiding idea and intervening in reality with its help to change this. (Figure 6, part H) This takes place as follows: when a reality of any kind whatsoever is subjected to speculative logic, this changes the

142 Reichertz 1999: 54.
143 Peirce 1958: 7.219.

perspective on this reality. The changed perspective inevitably influences how reality is understood, and, correspondingly, how it should be altered. The vanishing point thereby is the benefit that the newly developed, speculative logic contributes to practice. Can the new logic be applied? Is it capable of sensibly guiding future action? Does the new task definition inspire good solutions to problems? Does it open up new potential? Does it find or invent resources? Can it unleash a guiding idea? Can reality be positively altered in this way? Once again using the example in Zurich North, the new perspective of reality, meaning the fragmented urban landscape, creates new problems, potentials and design approaches. The focus of attention is thereby shifted to the infrastructure corridors. They can now either be spatially celebrated as elements providing orientation or be overcome with coverings and bridges, or public spaces and important collective uses, such as stadiums or parks, can be attached to the infrastructures. The new speculative logic will be left in effect for as long as it is helpful for the design task. When its assistance becomes limited, differentiations must take place. The thesis is abandoned when it proves useless.

The chapter on abduction can be summarized in four findings. First, design has both a protoabductive and an abductive effect. The specific abduction form of the design connects both modes of action, in order to satisfactorily address the generative potential of design with the abduction. This specific form is covered in the lower half of Figure 6. (Figure 6, lower half)

Secondly, it should be noted that the abduction develops theses that can be both scientifically verified or falsified, as well as practically applied and tested. Viewed thus, the empirical checking and the designing further development are two different tests that the speculatively formulated logic needs to pass before its comprehensibility is proven. The concept propagated by Schön of design as the simultaneous "use and testing" of a "guiding idea" thus finds its dual continuation here. (Figure 6, G)

Third, it becomes evident that, in addition to Peirce's triadic cognitive logic, consisting of abduction, deduction and induction, (Figure 6, C–F) a second triad exists, the triadic design logic. (Figure 6, A–C and G–H) This consists of the protoabductive creation of new consciousness, the creation of a speculative thesis originating from this, and the use and testing of this thesis. The interface of both triads is the abduction. A thesis regarding reality is posited in both triads. While the thesis is empirically tested in Peirce's cognitive triad, and should thus lead to new and reliable knowledge, theses for practical use in design are utilized in the design triad as a generative force for the examination and changing of reality, so to speak. The claim of Marcel Meili, which states that "the speculative, tentative and vague character of theses, their temporary inability to verify programmatic intentions or theoretical claims" when designing primarily manufactures "room to maneuver", can be contextualized at this point.[144] Together, the two triads form something like a *double loop of knowledge creation*. In the process, experimental and heuristic patterns of the design triad are combined with the empirical checks of the cognitive triad. In this connection, it should be added that both empirical testing and experimental use test the posited theses, and thus both manufacture critical inferences to reality. The two parts of this double loop cannot do without one another. Quite the opposite: they occupy complementary roles in the production of knowledge and impact one another reciprocally. While the cognitive triad generates the most reliable statements possible, (Figure 6, Episteme[145]), design assumes the tentative and speculative role of finding the thesis, forming the thesis and of using and testing the thesis in practice. (Figure 6, Praxis[146]) Both loops, thus both the triadic cognitive logic and the triadic design logic, each produce their own inferences to reality. These inferences in turn create new initial situations, which are fed into both loops. The two patterns of thought combine in this way. Speculation and testing exponentiate one another, and praxis and episteme propel themselves in the *double loop of knowledge creation*. When one pursues this pattern of thought, the creating of knowledge becomes an activity that links designing, speculative thought with empirical, testing thought through an iterative double loop. Figure 6 represents this *double loop of knowledge creation*. (Figure 6) Supported in this

144 Meili 2006.
145 Aristotle [335 B.C.] 1976: 1139–1141.
146 Ibid

context is Schleiermacher's statement, already introduced elsewhere, that the art of inventing wants to become science and the science of the found wants to become art, and that the greatest perfection only prevails in the marriage of contexts of discovery and reasoning.[147]

Fourth, it becomes noticeable how the examining and the changing dimensions of design have a reciprocal effect on one another: the examining dimension of design generates a new understanding of reality via the detour of the thought experiment and speculative logic, which in turn changes the normative goals and the strategies of the designer or design team. Design changes design – another iterative loop is thus completed, and proof is provided that the examining dimension of design strongly influences the changing dimension. The change and the examination are thereby not only products of design, but instead produce, as the substance and the cognitive vehicle, the initial situation for the subsequent design action. They are at the same time products and resources of design. Schön's "[...] experiment, which serves to generate [...] a new understanding of the phenomenon and a change in the situation", accordingly becomes the self-propelling *modus operandi* of design, the iterative motor.

---

147 Schleiermacher [1814] 1989: 5.

3
Design as experience

Although each specific situation is unique and correspondingly calls for individual consideration with respect to treatment, design operations are based on experience.[148] From the accumulation of many concrete and unique design tasks, a long-term perspective oriented to a general idea of the world arises, which ranges across projects through the entire career of a designer or design team. It sustains itself from the accumulation of various concrete designs, the resulting wealth of experience and the gradual sense of increasing knowledge. Despite all claims to the contrary, design does not start in a vacuum, but instead makes use of the already given and develops it further.[149] Schön describes the relationship between the specific site and the wealth of experience as follows:

> When a practitioner makes sense of a situation he perceives to be unique, he sees it as something already present in his repertoire. To see this site as that one is not to subsume the first under a familiar category or rule. It is, rather, to see the unfamiliar, unique situation as both similar to and different from the familiar one, without at first being able to say similar or different with respect to what. The familiar situation functions as a precedent, or a metaphor, or [...] an exemplar for the unfamiliar one.[150]

Design is thus something that resorts to the cultural repertoire of existing designs, but at the same time presents itself as something new.[151] For Schön, it is not about forcing a well-trodden schema onto a new situation. This would in fact be damaging, because the specific potential of every fundamentally unique situation would thereby be suppressed. It is much more the case that the specific properties and conditions of each situation should be uncovered, potential invented and that, building upon this, customized projects should be developed from the given circumstances. This happens – and this is where Schön's concept gets interesting – not in a space free of experience, but instead on the basis of constant comparison with existing experiences. These experiences are both used and changed through design and brought into new contexts. For Schön, the existing experience thus functions as a basis on which new actions, and

148 See Aristotle [335 B.C.] 1976: 1139–1141.
149 Ammon 2015: 187.
150 Schön 1983: 138.
151 List 2009: 326.
152 Cassirer [1925] 1994: II 187.
153 List 2009: 327.
154 Schön 1983: 138.
155 See Smith [2001] 2011.
156 The prime matter of this repertoire, according to the philosopher Mark Johnson, is composed of "embodied schemata" (Johnson 1987: 29), thus physically experienceable patterns, which are perceived pre-reflectively and even prior to any conceptualization, meaning without having to take the detour of language, as regularities. They originate from the human movements in space and describe situations, such as "being inside", "being contained" or "emerging" (Ibid: 37, see Ungers [1981] 2011). Designers develop much more complex patterns from these primal schemes, for example, in the case of the hotel, the pattern of

thus also new experiences, can occur. The concept of "experience" is thus not only anchored as a wealth of experience in the past but is also based in the present as an inquisitive experiment in the sense of something to be newly discovered. This thing to be newly discovered is very similar to the "experiencing" ("Erleben", living through something) of Cassirer, already described above. He too sees the focus on doing, "from which the mental organization of reality takes its starting point for human beings".[152] Added to this is the fact that each new experience changes the existing wealth of experience and thus also influences future actions. The process of design, the act of design must of course resort to certain procedures, forms, practices and stocks of knowledge. However, to become design as the creation of something new, it must also violate, go beyond this process. According to the aesthetician, Elisabeth List, this is a moment of uncertainty and of change. Existing forms are thereby not only used, but also adapted, transformed and overcome.[153] As a potential increase in knowledge, experiencing in the sense of discovering is thus also oriented to the future as "the new" in the form of a constantly changing "repertoire".[154]

Repertoires as experience products of design

As Mark K. Smith stresses in his account of Schön's theory, the "repertoire" is a key concept for Schön. "Practitioners build up a repertoire: a collection of images, ideas, examples and actions that they can draw upon".[155] These repertoires are collections of recurring patterns and orders that characterize action and perceptions.[156] Because, significantly, the establishing of a repertoire does not follow standardized techniques either: the planning theoretician, Bent Flyvbjerg, has determined that "not rules, but instead thousands of examples, comparative, direct and intuitively based on experience"[157] are applied in the process. As "holistic patterns",[158] these countless examples are compared with each new situation for commonalities and differences. With regard to this, Dreyfus and Dreyfus developed the concept of "arationality",[159] which Flyvbjerg uses to better

"the slope in the blazing evening light of the reflecting sea, with fir scented pines". The sophistication of these highly developed, verbalized patterns, which form the expanded repertoire of practitioners, cannot, however, conceal the fact that these are ultimately rooted in physically experienced, "embodied schemata" (see Blumenberg 2006, List 2009).
157 Flyvbjerg 2001: 21, Dreyfus and Dreyfus 1988: XII.
158 Flyvbjerg 2001: 20.
159 Dreyfus 1988: 36.

outline this intuitive, "virtuous action".[160] He determined that arational behavior, entirely in contrast with rational behavior, describes situation-contingent behavior, which occurs without conscious analytical division of the overall situation into individual elements, and without evaluation according to rules independent of context. Arational behavior is complementary to rationality and involves contextual weighing, evaluations, trial and error, experiences, common sense, intuition, sensory impressions and practical knowledge. Over time, an operative collection of patterns "based on experience" – or in other words, a repertoire – can be reflexively created for practice.[161]

With the emphasis of the repertoire as a product of action and reflection, Schön creates an explicit link to the cognitive representations of the philosopher, John Dewey, which are presented in *How We Think* and provide the impetus for many of Schön's concepts.[162] Dewey describes the difference between the application of rules in the sense of scientific principles and a reflective practice that cannot be understood in deductive rules due to its inconsistency and complexity.[163] He concludes from this that practice calls for an independent form of knowledge, and that this form must be differentiated from the principles of epistemic science independent of context.[164] Dewey finds such a form of knowledge in practice with Aristotle: "phronesis".[165] Aristotle describes "phronesis" as the actual foundation of practice and defines this form of knowledge as a specific type of wisdom relevant to practical action, implying both good judgement and excellence of character and habits, sometimes referred to as "practical virtue". According to Aristotle, "phronesis" is an "attitude based on deliberation [...] that guides action in the field of what is good or bad for human beings".[166] It is not a "knowledge of general principles only: it must also take account of particular facts, since it is concerned with action, and action deals with particular things."[167] Aristotle further differentiates "phronesis" from "episteme", which encompasses factual knowledge, and from "techne", which involves technical or artisanal ability.[168] In keeping with this tradition of thought, design is an art that, beyond the epistemologically ascertained facts and technical

160 Bourdieu 1972: 8, 15.
161 Alexander et al. 1977: IX–XVIII.
162 Dewey 1910: 30, 66, 78, 120–125, see Dewey 1903, 1925, 1929.
163 Gänshirt 2011: 30, see Dorst 2003, Lawson and Dorst 2009.
164 Ibid
165 Like Dewey, Schön, Dreyfus and Flyvbjerg also appeal to Aristotle's fundamental concept of "phronesis". See Healey 2009b: 277–292.
166 Aristotle [335 B.C.] 1976: 1139.
167 Ibid, see Ebert 1995: 167.
168 Flyvbjerg 2001: 22–23, 54.

or artisanal ability, is to a central extent dependent upon personal knowledge based on action and experience: on phronetic knowledge. This knowledge is necessary to be capable of action in complicated and controversial situations. Accordingly, the actual problem of design is a problem of practice, a problem of good and reasonable action. The evaluation of a principally insoluble, wicked problem is thus elevated to a central problem of design.[169] It feeds on processed, ordered experience.[170] "Phronesis" thus calls for practical experience, and this in turn originates from design or, more generally, from doing, from experiencing and from undergoing.

As already suggested, the experience finds its way into the "repertoire"[171] of the designer in the form of "holistic patterns"[172]. From this, it can be compared as an analogy with each new situation for similarities and differences. It is, so to speak, the wealth of experience that can be accessed when designing.

Three categories of repertoires can be differentiated in design. They derive from Schön's idea of the design operation, which both changes and an examines reality:[173]

Repertoire I: DESIGN OPERATIONS
Tools of targeted irritation; achieved through designing itself

Repertoire II: SITUATIONS
Types of reality; achieved through the examining dimension of design

Repertoire III: STRATEGIES
Ways of realization; achieved through the changing dimension of design

Repertoire I encompasses the design operations. It is fed from the design experience to the extent that the designer experiences certain experiments as successful, bundles these and stores them as a collection in their memory, so to speak. For a subsequent design task, this can be drawn upon as a comparison and be either adapted, used or rejected. The seaside hotel once again serves as an example here: the "rotating of the building transverse with the main alignment" becomes a building block

169 See Forester 1989, 2009, Flyvbjerg 1998.
170 Oechslin 2012b: 585.
171 Schön 1983: 138.
172 Flyvbjerg 2001: 20.
173 Ibid: 85.

in the repertoire of design operations. In the example in Zurich North, the transfer experiment, thus the "transfer of a known urban pattern to an unknown situation" is the type of operation that can be applied again in a different context – especially as a thought experiment for its examination.

Repertoire II, which collects situations, arises from the examining dimension of the design operation. These are similar types of reality, which are encountered again and again. In the hotel example, the "plot located on the wooded slope transverse with the ocean" is just such a situation. The "plot lying transverse with the main view" may eventually be stored in one's memory as an even more general situation type. In the example in Zurich North, the situation was examined through a transfer experiment and described as a situation type with "plot at the urban periphery surrounded by infrastructure corridors". Existing situations are of course often much more complex because one also has to take other things like building law, constructional, socio-economic and psychological aspects into account.[174] In the process, various situation types are applied in combination, and not as a set of rules, but instead as a mesh of associations.

Repertoire III, which encompasses strategies, results from the changing dimension of design. It bundles types of realizations, which, experience has shown, can be successfully applied in certain situations. In the example of the seaside hotel, the "prong-shaped ground plan geometry" can be viewed as a promising realization within the situation type of "plot lying transverse with the main view".

These three repertoires are closely related and cross fertilize each other. This should be demonstrated with the example of the hotel design. The "plot lying transverse with the main view" should become visible through the design of a slab at the seaside. It is a situation type from Repertoire II. This in turn calls for a new design action: the "rotating of the building transverse with the main alignment", an operation type from Repertoire I. The action of rotating generates a new consciousness of reality: the "plot located on the wooded slope", thus a situation type from Repertoire II. This new situation provokes further design

---

174 See Boucsein 2014.

operations from Repertoire I, through which the "prong-shaped ground plan geometry" arises, which should in turn be assigned to Repertoire III.

The countless design operations are the experience resource of this process. The establishing of the repertoire takes place through this, inductively and with typification. Internal discussions within our discipline made clear that these repertoires, very similar to the examining dimension of design, are in fact implicitly welcome side effects of alert designers. They have often been described as "gifts". However, as unexposed aspects of design, they all too often vanish from the theoretical discourse. They mostly flow unconsciously into the design calculation.

Some repertoires tend to find their way into the architectural and urban planning discourse more often than others. Because Repertoire II (situations of reality) and Repertoire III (strategies of realization), in contrast with Repertoire I (design operations), are products of the designing action they are more easily perceived by designers than the mostly unconsciously applied design operations. They thus tend to be used more for comparisons, typification and theoretical classifications. Functioning as examples for these repertoires are, among others, Kees Christiaanse's *Situation*[175] for Repertoire II, in which various urban situations are presented ordered as spatial-cultural types, and the collected writings entitled *A Matter of Things* by Manuel Solà-Morales for Repertoire III, which reflexively structure his decades of design activity and typify these into three different strategies for implementation.[176] As already mentioned, Repertoire I is not as easy to comprehend. It is imprinted much more deeply into design itself. For this reason in particular, the first repertoire category should be examined and fully differentiated below: Repertoire I (design operations), out of which the two other repertoires grow. This consists of those designs that have "not only an informing [...] but also a transforming and enlightening impact on the respective "reality".[177]

---

175 See Christiaanse et al. 2005.
176 See Solà-Morales 2008, Kretz and Salewski 2014: 177.
177 Pfisterer 2011: 372.

Repertoires as stimuli for design

Repertoires are not only ordering reservoirs of similar isolated occurrences, but instead also stimulate the wealth of experience of the designer and cause experimental changes to the examined situation as a result. In his book *L'architettura della città* [The Architecture of the City], Italian architect and theoretician Aldo Rossi discovered a tool for such a stimulating repertoire, which he explicitly names "type".[178] Rossi defines type as the shared core of various similar individual cases, or, expressed metaphorically, the shared DNA that defines their relatedness. Rossi's types are "holistic patterns" that crystallize from the individual experience and, according to Rossi, much more so from the "collective memory" of a society.[179] Rossi thus emphasizes in this context that the type is a cultural fact, and not an absolute constant. Rossi presents the "Alley of the Washerwomen" as an example of such a "cultural type".[180] (Figure 7) This "Alley of the Washerwomen" is, as a type, a back alley in a densely inhabited city, which is austere and spatially narrow, and which serves as rear access both for servants and for infrastructural matters, such as trash disposal and deliveries. The façades have many French windows and balconies for hanging laundry to dry. The alley smells like soap and wet cloth and echoes with conversations of the washerwomen and cries of the errand boys. In order to differentiate the type from the individual case, Rossi presents examples from various South European cities (Milan in Italy, Seville and Viana in Spain), which are similar in their basic principles and together form this cultural type. Rossi defines the connecting basic principle as follows: "The word *type* represents [...] the idea of an element [...] their origins and primary causes".[181] It is therefore not absolutely necessary that exactly the same scent of soap prevails in every "alley", but the principal spatial-societal idea as a narrow back alley and secondary opening without a representative function should.

178 Rossi 1966: 40.
179 See Halbwachs [1939] 1950.
180 Rossi 1966: 38–39.
181 Ibid: 40.

Figure 7.
Typological Questions: Alley of the Washerwomen
(Rossi [1966] 1982)

Such a cultural type is accordingly neither a frozen aesthetic picture nor a geometric control diagram that one should simply copy without questioning, but instead a principle consisting of the material object and the societal role. According to Rossi, "a particular type is associated with a particular form and way of life".[182] The cultural type thereby links various aspects of habitat, thus psychological, societal, living and material facts and is thus something like a culturally anchored "social-material scheme".[183] This social-material scheme can be accessed for new design actions, not as a blueprint, but instead as a principle, as a metaphor or as an idea. Peter Eisenman refers to the potency of the Rossi type for stimulating design in his foreword to the English translation, in which he stresses the processual side of the type:

182 Ibid
183 See Johnson 1987.

Rossi discovers in Typology the possibility of invention precisely because type is both process and object. [...] As a process, Type contains a synthetic character [...]. It is an object-apparatus that analyzes and also invents.[184]

The type is thus both the memory of that undergone, that experienced, as well as the basis for the new, that still to come. At this point if not before, it becomes clear that repertoires are not a collection of prefabricated solutions but are instead the interfaces between memory and imagination. Repertoires should thus instead be better understood as a fund, which impacts the respective newly occurring situation in the form of types, analogies, metaphors, images and ideas.[185] In the chaos of perceptions, they on the one hand create possible orders using familiar patterns. The previously unordered wealth of data is thus structured, and the countless individual manifestations are incorporated into a well-known structure of meaning. On the other hand, however, these illustrative types, analogies, metaphors, images and ideas also stimulate new thoughts, reactions and actions and thus reveal innovative potential.[186] This results in new structures of meaning. The type, correctly applied, thus has a dual function: Structure formation and innovation. The type thus becomes a tool, which both manufactures orders and propels speculative design.

Eisenman specifies in order to more precisely narrow down the specific type of innovation: "Type allows for transformations [...] which are prearranged but still unforeseeable".[187] The "transformations" referred to are thus unforeseeable in keeping with this but are by all means prestructured. The creative innovative potential, for which designers are mainly praised and admired, is, according to Eisenman, not an invention from out of the blue. On the contrary, it is nourished from the wealth of experience and its targeted confrontation with each new situation, involving a process of transformation. Design must thus resort to certain patterns, but in order to become design as a creation of the new, it must violate and transgress these patterns. Existing forms are thereby not only used, but also broken down.[188] The

184 Eisenman 1982: 8.
185 See Ungers 1982.
186 Pehnt 2011: 178, Ungers 1980: 23, see Schwarz 1960.
187 Eisenman 1982: 5.
188 List 2009: 327.

creative, experimental search for the unknown, specific and unique is thus principally not dialectically directed against the idea of the type. On the contrary, they cause one another and exist in a state of precise mutual dependence.

They are held together by the concept of the selective and plastic wealth of experience. This wealth of experience originates from an experienced past, thus influences the present and is constantly changed and expanded by it; it is therefore plastic. It is selective because it only retains those empirical values that appear significant to the designer or design team. The projective potential of the experienced past can thus be stimulated using similar experiences, summarized in repertoires or types:

Through the apparatus of Type [...] memory can imagine and reconstruct a future time of fantasy. This memory is set into motion through the inventive potential of the typological apparatus, the analogous design process.[189]

As explained in the section concerning design as examination, analogies are heuristic methods and accordingly serve not only the discovery of new knowledge, but also as repertoires that stimulate designs. Eisenman refers to the latter when he describes the "inventive potential of the typological apparatus".

Another excellent overview of the analyses and typology of the targeted irritation can be found in the early writings and structures of Peter Eisenman.[190] Eisenman examined basal operations, which, in his opinion, are possible in the Cartesian realm for the transformation of a platonic body: shifting, rotating, multiplication, etc.[191] In the process, he documented the formal transformation processes and used these on the one hand to develop projects and, on the other, to examine the basic conditions and limits of the Cartesian-geometric space. Eisenman accordingly attempts, first, to delimit an operative repertoire and, secondly, to query the operations concerning their changing and examining dimensions. (Figure 8)

---

189 Eisenman 1982: 10.
190 See Eisenman [1963] 2006, 1978, 2008.
191 Moneo 2005: 160.

Figure 8.
Diagram matrix for the House IV
project (Eisenman 1971)

In this context, it is worth noting the observation of architecture theoretician Jörg Gleiter that Eisenman recognized potential for critical practice in automation and processuality:

> *Eisenman's early architectural practice was distinguished by the diagrammatic automation of the design processes and their strict processualization, which applied the seriality of machine production to the design process itself. The goal here was to propel the design processes to that point where, by always using the same operation, the serialized, rational processes turn into highly labyrinthine structures and the overdetermined rationality into overdetermined sensual impact.*[192]

Once again it becomes clear that the creative innovation potential, ascribed to the overdetermined sensual impact, arises from a

---

192 Gleiter 2008: 63.

process of transformation – and not *ex nihilo*. Consequently, design always falls back on the given and develops it further.[193] Both Rossi's analogies and Eisenman's transformation experiments are typical processes of qualitative heuristics.[194] With reference to the repertoires, it is conspicuous that Rossi's and Eisenman's processes possess a doubly intertwined function: on the one hand, this gain in knowledge is illuminated, which occurs when designing in a concrete situation by consulting with the existing repertoire of experience. On the other, the repertoire is supplemented and expanded with new insights through the newly acquired experience of designing. In this process repertoires become more and more refined and precise.

After presenting the three repertoires as experience products of design in this section and examining Repertoire I in more detail, the three repertoire categories can now be summarized as experience products of design: Experience Repertoire I encompasses design operations as tools of the targeted irritation. It is achieved through the design operation. Experience Repertoire II bundles strategies which can change reality. This is achieved through the changing dimension. Experience Repertoire III contains situations of reality. This is achieved through the examining dimension.

Summing up we can thus draw the following three conclusions:

First, all three of the experience repertoires mentioned can originate from the designing experiment, typifiable knowledge with regard to the experiment types – as tools of examination (Repertoire I: design operations), typifiable knowledge with regard to the usable concepts and strategies of qualification of the examined reality (Repertoire II: strategies) and finally typifiable knowledge with regard to the qualities of the examined reality (Repertoire III: situations).

Second, it can be concluded that the repertoires are the pivotal hinges between the individual case and the wealth of experience: by bundling similar phenomena, experiments and strategies they produce both a rich fund of typical patterns for practice and the reference system for further theoretical endeavors. Repertoires are accordingly both toolboxes and memory.

193 Ammon 2015: 187.
194 See Kühne: 2005.

Through their pivotal function, they occupy a prominent position in the methodologies of design.[195] Third, relating to Donald Schön's "use/test entity" and complementing this: design as an iterative activity functions not only as a vehicle for projective change *(changing dimension)* and as an examination tool of the existing reality *(examining dimension)*, but also as a source for the wealth of experience across situations. The three repertoires of design originate from this wealth of experience.[196] The window to the third dimension of design is opened through the experience: the *ordering dimension*, which synthesizes the acquired knowledge and transfers it into a "theory of practice". This third dimension will be presented in the following chapter.

---

195 See Rossi 1966, Alexander 1977, Lynch 1981, Schön 1983.
196 Schön 1983: 138.

4
Design as theory of practice

Up to now, we have shown how to deal with concrete, contradictory and ambiguous problems when designing and have discussed which role transformative interventions, analogies and experience play in this. It has also been determined that each concrete situation requires specific knowledge, its own perspective and thus also a tailored solution. The concrete processing of such a task is mostly too complex, too expansive and too futuristic for it to be organized, structured and thus handled without forward-thinking speculative activities.[197] Design is necessary for this.

Subsequently, one can draw two conclusions here: first, the respective concrete situation defines the knowledge required. Practice is the compass that provides direction in the unclear diversity of all possible "should knows" and "must knows".[198] Secondly, it follows from this that the work required here involves weakly determined processes that can only be vaguely defined in advance. Designers who occupy themselves with concrete problems are hardly helped by generally valid schemata or absolute rules, because, with such formulas, there is a danger of losing touch with the reality in which the project should ultimately come into being.[199] Bruno Taut's view that rigid rules of proportion are not only senseless, but even harmful, goes right to the heart of this.[200] Instead, differentiated knowledge of possibilities for action in concrete situations is required for design. On the one hand, these of course encompass the sensible use of tools as creativity and realization techniques. However, technique alone is not enough. As already explained, Aristotle describes "phronesis" as the actual foundation of practice. The actual problem of design is thus not only a question of doing, but primarily that of good and reasonable action (thus of "praxis" and of "phronesis").[201] Different from in the natural sciences, which often see themselves as value-free striving for irrefutable knowledge ("episteme") to the greatest extent possible, according to Gänshirt, "the question of value, of the value of a piece of knowledge, of a skill, an action or a tool, is of central importance [...] when dealing with design".[202] Not unlike jurisprudence, weighing-up an action in a complex

197 Gänshirt 2011: 57, see Ammon 2015: 187–188.
198 Fischer 1999: 74.
199 Oechslin 2012a: 588.
200 Windelband 1904: 4–27, Taut [1935–36] 2009: 52–53.
201 Aristotle [335 B.C.] 1976: 1139–1141.
202 Gänshirt 20: 22–23.

case may be a matter of experience (*empeiria*), but it requires more than just accumulated comparative designs. But how is it possible to act in a balanced way in concrete terms if no generally valid scheme or unquestionable logic can be applied? This is where jurisprudence can help out, not only as a metaphor, but also as a comparison worthy of investigation. Based on specific precedents and theoretical constructs of a more general nature, jurisprudence shows in an exemplary way how, through long-term examination of many different concrete, mostly ambiguous and contradictory facts, both case collections on the one hand – obviously via detours – and justifiable and evaluable generalizations (such as human rights) on the other can be made. The case collections correspond to the repertoires from which precedents (or prototypes) are repeatedly drawn; the generalizations correspond to the creation of theory in the designing disciplines. However, why generalizations for practice at all; to what purpose theory in "phronesis"? In *Der Architekt als Theoretiker* [The Architect as Theoretician] architecture historian Werner Oechslin warns that lack of theory risks lack of judgement, as the designer would simply be overwhelmed by reality without the structure provided by prior knowledge.[203] The absence of theory is an ideal of many artists or scientists because they wish to expose themselves "to the totality of living existence" in order to "absorb the world without the filter of theoretical categories".[204] Fernando Pessoa's phrase "... the sacred instinct of having no theories..."[205] is, according to Gänshirt, a prime example of this which describes the freedom of humanity that Karl Jaspers once characterized as the "existence of freedom inaccessible to all research".[206] Freedom manifests itself in, among other things, the creative act of design. Conscious of this ideal, Oechslin at the same time counters it by referring to the opposite ideal: the indisputable rule.[207] Both ideals are, in keeping with their natures, inadequate extremes, and it is of key importance to assert oneself between them. In order to tackle questions like "What is the problem?", "What is the goal?", "What knowledge is required?", "Which method is appropriate?" and "How can the relationship with reality

203 Oechslin 2012a: 855.
204 Gänshirt 2011: 16.
205 Pessoa [1933] 1991: 77.
206 Jaspers [1923] 1980: 50.
207 Oechslin 2012b: 585.

be maintained?", it would make no sense simply to reject the opposite extreme and not query the empirical values collected within it.

The primacy of realization

As discussed in the previous section, neither absolute freedom nor rigid rules provide sensible instruments for design. It is key here not to become lost in the broad field between the absence of theory and rules carved in stone. We can first look to Vitruvius here, who proclaimed practice as a compass.[208] Oechslin follows this lead and finds Schinkel's concepts of "activity" and "realization",[209] which should guide designers. According to the architect Karl Friedrich Schinkel, it is particularly realization that provides orientation. The goal of realization is namely a social-material artefact, toward which the design work, including its guiding ideas and theories, can be oriented. In order to manufacture such an artefact, certain approaches are required, and specific stocks of knowledge are necessary, but not all. This varies depending upon the task and context. Through its orientation to an artefact, the primacy of realization thus defines the field of knowledge that should flow into the design calculation. This is not infinite but instead limited by the specific task. To return to the hotel design again, knowledge, for example, of the constructional anchoring of the hotel in the slope, of functional processes of facility management and of the aesthetic and ecological embedding of the hotel in the sparse pine forest on the coast is required, but not knowledge about building in water or about laws for high-rises. At the same time, the knowledge required for design is unstable across projects: it changes with the task, the degree of experience of the designer or design team and the technical development. A hotel design by the sea requires at least partially different expertise to a high-rise design in a densely populated city. The realization of a specific solution, an artefact, however, defines not only the stocks of knowledge required, but also the direction of the knowledge creation, meaning the method of understanding. Because a specific social-material situation is usually found at the beginning

208 Fischer 1999: 74.
209 Oechslin 2012b: 585.

of design, the creation of knowledge initially progresses from the specific case to the more general. This occurs, for example, by problematizing, comparing, thematizing, drawing conclusions by analogy, typifying and categorizing to finally flow into the repertoire of the designer or design team. Remaining with the example of the hotel design, the student initially determines through the observation of the location by the sea, and subsequently through concrete design experiments, that the project is better arranged orthogonally to the beach on the plot available to it. Despite this disadvantageous arrangement, an ocean view should be made possible for all guests. Now that the design problem has been found, it is helpful to study similar hotel complexes and to compare these with one's own design task. In the process, recurrent features may become apparent. For example, the fact that almost all designs both featuring rooms with an ocean view and arranged orthogonally to the beach have stepped or staggered façades. Through this observation, the student creates the ordering category "building, positioned orthogonally to the beach with sea view" and collects transferable concepts within this category that have convincingly used staggered or stepped façades as possible solutions. (Figure 9)

Figure 9.
Famous examples of staggered buildings:
The Shell-Haus in Berlin and the Salk Institute in La Jolla,
California (Fahrenkamp 1930–1932, Kahn 1962–1963)

The available concepts are now used and tested in the hotel design. Of key importance here is to re-concretize and test the gradually ordered knowledge in the individual case. This gradual transfer from the concrete to the general (and back), as seen in the example of the hotel design, contrasts with unbridgeable schisms like "concrete vs. general", "science vs. art", "practice vs. theory" and "hand vs. head". Instead, a smooth mediation or constant reshaping should be presumed. As determined by de Bruyn, it is precisely "the coequal occupation with calculating and painting" that leads to the "reconciliation of theory and practice, manual and mental work" when designing.[210] This gradual transfer from the practical to the theoretical (and back) with the goal of evident realization ultimately defines which theory is sensible for design: A theory of practice. According to Hungarian philosopher Kristof Nyiri, knowledge is first and foremost practical and only secondarily theoretical. Knowledge thus means knowing how, meaning ability, doing, realizing. Theory, therefore, does not become detached from practice, but instead a tool for realization: "Theory is one of the instruments of action, of practice, similar to our other instruments, tools, devices".[211] The rediscovery of the profoundly practical nature of knowledge is an accomplishment of the 20th century and particularly came to light in the works of Wittgenstein and Heidegger.[212] The language philosopher, Gilbert Ryle, also comes to the conclusion in *The Concept of Mind* that "knowing that" dissolves in "knowing how", and infers from this that: "theorizing is one practice amongst others".[213] These orientation aids just described, which result from an orientation to "practice", "activity" or even to "realization", lead from the ad hoc solution through repeated use of similar cases through the wealth of experience to ordered knowledge, thus to the theory of practice, in order to then be brought, ordered, reflected upon and evaluated, back into reality. This transformation process from reality via theory back to practice, as just outlined, can be described as the *ordering dimension of design*.

---

210 de Bruyn 2008: 113, see Alberti [approx. 1443-1452] 1485.
211 Nyiri 2004: 157.
212 See Wittgenstein 1921, Heidegger [1927] 2001.
213 Ryle 1949: 16.

Open-ended abduction and induction: thematization and typification

Now that the pattern of thought of realization and its consequences for a theory of practice have been explained, we ask what methods this procedure might call for. Are there describable procedures that can gradually extract important observations and themes from the multifariousness of reality and condense these into principles and applicable patterns that can be represented? This question can be addressed using the famous example of Le Corbusier and Pierre Jeanneret's *Cinq points de l'architecture moderne*[214] [The Five Points of a New Architecture], which the two architects postulated in 1927 as a manifesto decisively impacting modern architecture. (Figure 10)

The five points are represented in the left column as components of a "new architecture". The right column presents a comparison with a typical house of the 19th century.

First, Le Corbusier and Jeanneret describe the method for theory creation by stating: "These are the theoretical conclusions of successive observations made on building sites for several years".[215] Practical activity and construction site experience of many years are thus the substance from which the observed phenomena are successively condensed into comprehensible principles. This is followed by "The theoretical exposition leads to the simplicity of the formula".[216] They are thus concerned with an ultimately elegant and simple synthesis of their observations, or, more precisely, of their prolonged processing of experience over many years. In this process of gradual understanding, the authors use the methods of thematization and typification. Both methods will be discussed in more detail below.

The thematization contains the shaping of themes and properties from the world of appearances that appear relevant and thus plot the framework of the design. Key here is to abductively place the phenomenon in a new relationship or context, to name relevant themes, to problematize these and to evaluate them. Le Corbusier and Jeanneret name columns, rooftop gardens, open ground plans and façades, as well as ribbon windows as

214 Le Corbusier and Jeanneret [1923] 1927.
215 Ibid: 208. Quotes from this publication translated from the French by Simon Kretz.
216 Ibid

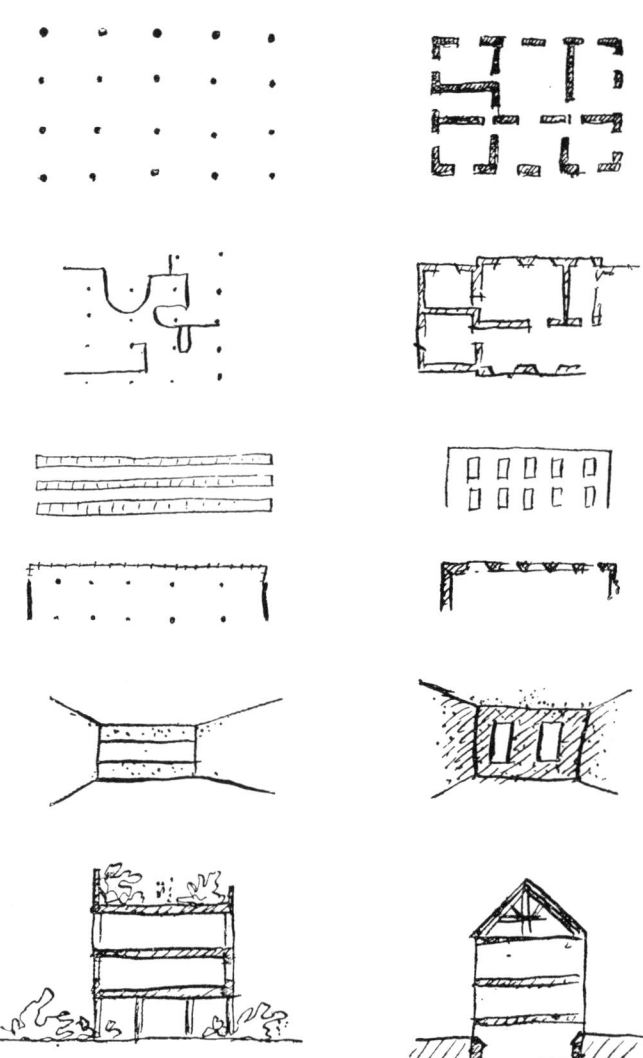

Fig. 10.
"The Five Points of a New Architecture"
(Le Corbusier and Jeanneret [1923] 1927)

five points for a future architecture, (Fig. 10, left-hand column) because they, in their opinion, synthesize and represent central technical, ethical and aesthetic *topoi* of modernity, for example, the potency of reinforced concrete as a new material, the wish for more (social) hygiene, the automobile as an emerging means of mobility, the banishing of the mythical, the asymmetric composition theories and the bucolic imagining of nature. The architect and theoretician, Christopher Alexander, described this as follows:

A well-designed house [...] illuminates the problem of [...] what the context is, and thereby clarifies the life which it accommodates. Thus Le Corbusier's invention of new house forms in the 1920s really represented part of the modern attempt to understand the twentieth century's new way of life.[217]

Accordingly, the five points apply not only as five elements of a derivation of the new manner of design and as a reaction to changing usage needs, but also as sensually perceptual representations and vehicles of cultivation that had been tested for their modernity and positively evaluated.[218] This achievement of synthesis of Le Corbusier and Jeanneret sheds lights on the tightly entangled interrelationships of perception, judgement and conceptualization. It also provides a targeted guiding thread through the jungle of possible perceptions, associations, conjectures and judgements. Closely based on Schinkel's claim that "in art, thought must always be directed towards realization, and in representation the critique (judgement) necessarily inherent in the creative spirit becomes visible",[219] the five points of Le Corbusier and Jeanneret re-concretize the theory of modernity and provide instruction for further realization.

The typification contains the inductive search for similar constellations and their examination regarding analogies and differences. The authors typify the "conclusions of successive observations" into five architectural elements and compare the new properties of these elements through a typological comparison with a typical house from the 19th century, in this case aiming only at establishing difference. (Fig. 10, right-hand column)

217 Alexander 1964: 91.
218 See Vitruvius [33–22 B.C.] 1981, Vogt 1996.
219 Schinkel, in Peschken 1979: 34. Quote translated from the German by Simon Kretz.

More general statements valid across cases can thus be made and, for this reason, specific instructions for action can be provided for a concrete solution to the problem of building the homes of the future. It becomes obvious that they were primarily interested in guiding theory back to reality as reflected upon, ordered and evaluated knowledge and in allowing this to impact upon reality in the form of concise syntheses as a structuring element. The theory therefore procures competence, because it not only accumulates experiential and technical knowledge, but also orders, reflects upon and evaluates, and thus converts it into explicit principles, rules, points, criteria and systems. This knowledge in turn structures the evaluation of new situations and the design of possible futures.

With reference to Oechslin's thesis, it can thus be stated that located between the designing, realizing practice and the ordering theory is not only the already discussed experience but also the competence or, in other words, the power of judgement.[220] The most important provider of impulses for this line of thought is Immanuel Kant.[221] As stated by art philosopher Peter Osborne, Kant repeatedly emphasized that the most important property of art is anchored specifically in mediation between the aesthetics of a potentially endless reality and the logic of a coherent conceptualization.[222] Consequently, this contains translation processes in both directions, and thus both "cognitive experience" and "pre-conceptual synthesis", as well as the "realization of aesthetic ideas" and the "sensual representation of concepts".[223] Canadian epistemologist Lagueux pursues a very similar line of argumentation of reciprocal contingency and mediation when he sounds out the relationship of aesthetics and ethics in architecture. According to Lagueux, ethical problems are decisions that are intrinsic to architectural and aesthetic, and thus also ethical decisions.[224] Therefore, Lagueux also believes that design is an art of mediation which attempts to solve ethical problems by way of architectural decisions that are at the same time also solutions for aesthetic problems. Lagueux illustrates this as follows:

220 Oechslin 2012b: 585.
221 See Kant 1781.
222 Osborne 2014: 55.
223 Ibid; see Kant 1781, 1790.
224 Lagueux 2004: 130–133, see Valéry [1921] 1973.

Should the architect build houses that open onto public spaces or rather increase the intimacy of family life by reducing and concealing such openings? Should an architect enhance secrecy and individualism inside a dwelling or favor a family's collective life by way of large living and dining rooms? Should the shapes and the colors of buildings such as churches, schools, and hospitals awake sentiments of joy or invite profound meditation? Should libraries be conceived of as austere temples devoted only to scholarly research or be designed as attractively as possible in order to incite people from any educational background to use them?[225]

All these questions have clear ethical implications, but the architectural responses to them of course also have an aesthetic character. Lagueux thereby refers to a "quasi identity" between ethics and aesthetics in architecture.[226] A "critical judgement" gradually arises from the oscillating mediation of aesthetics and ethics, to which the philologist, Friedrich Creuzer, ascribes qualities like "logical incisiveness of thinking, the fineness of choice, the certainty of taste".[227] The "precisely differentiating" and adjudicating sense, thus the "separating critique must move to the center"[228] in order to be able to evaluate multifarious experiential values and continue to use them. This representation in turn coincides quite precisely with Aristotle's representation of "phronesis" as the specific form of knowledge of practical action.

Flexible patterns as encyclopedic vehicles

Oechslin ascribes further examples of the idea of a discerning theory of practice to Vignola's *Le cinque ordini dell'Architettura*[229] [The Five Orders of Architecture] and Gottfried Semper's categorization of the four architectural *Urelemente* [basic elements] in *Die vier Elemente der Baukunst*[230] [The Four Elements of Architecture]. An important, more recent example is Christopher Alexander's highly regarded collection *A Pattern Language*.[231] Forming its foundation were countless analyses of individual architectural and urban planning situations, which were categorized by Alexander and examined and discussed with regard to meaning and usage. (Figure 11)

---

225 Lagueux 2004: 118-119.
226 Ibid: 133.
227 Creuzer et al. 1805: 10.
228 Ibid
229 Vignola [1562] 1600: 10-13, see Oechslin 2012b: 581.
230 Semper 1851, see Semper 1860-1863.
231 Alexander et al. 1977.

32 SHOPPING STREET*

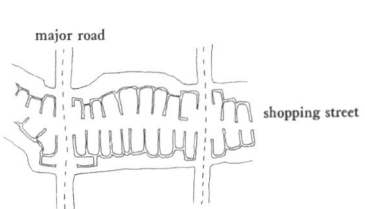

Figure 11.
Pattern 32: The Shopping Street
(Alexander et al. 1977)

The result was a detailed and richly illustrated, encyclopedic collection, a so-called "pattern language", containing evaluated and operatively usable situation types. With his extensive and sorted pattern language, Alexander created not only a methodology for an expandable theory of practice, but also reactivated the tradition of the encyclopedic ordering and processing of knowledge extending far back into the history of architecture. Entirely in contrast to the teleological and schismatic paradigm of modernity, this places new achievements in positions of equal importance with old and thus not only conceptualizes the simultaneity of the nonsimultaneous,[232] but also strives to advance a conception of the world that is as networked and coherent as possible.[233] For this reason, Alexander's patterns are not individually delimitable objects (like, for example, the house, traffic lights, seating benches or trees), but are instead related complexes such as the street corner or the shopping street. The latter contain both several objects and their interrelationships. These patterns thus occupy themselves more with habitats than with individual, contextless objects.[234] The various patterns are also not only carefully differentiated from one

232 See Schlögel 2003.
233 de Bruyn 2008: 193.
234 Burckhardt [1980] 2012: 13–14.

another and enumerated, but also refer to one another with various cross-references. Not only for Alexander do the cross-references perform a key function as media for the construction of the encyclopedic form of knowledge: Their use was already assigned a central role by Diderot and d'Alembert in their famous *Encyclopédie ou Dictionnaire raisonné des sciences, des arts et des métiers*[235] [Encyclopedia, or a Systematic Dictionary of the Sciences, Arts, and Crafts], because their function consisted of uniting the individual elements of knowledge into the most coherent network of knowledge possible.[236] The oft criticized pre-modern dream of classical encyclopedias, that a single mind could comprehend the entirety of knowledge, the so-called "harmonia mundi",[237] from all sides and coherently, had very much begun to falter from the 18th century if not before.[238] Not wishing to throw out the baby with the purifying bathwater, Novalis suggested around the turn of the 19th century that the no longer tenable, static concept of the comprehensive encyclopedia be dynamized and transformed into pluralistic, "encyclopedic" thinking.[239] According to Novalis, this is an "exponentiated encyclopedia" and does not primarily concern itself with the solid substance of knowledge, but instead with the "flexible patterns" that "bring the elements of knowledge into turbulence and make them fruitful in this new way".[240] For Novalis, these "flexible patterns" are of a "linguistic nature"[241] – from here, the path to Alexander's design-stimulating pattern language is not long. The pattern language can thus be comprehended as a post-modern extension of Novalis' encyclopedia, and is thus even closely related with other performative and dynamic networking tools like index boxes[242] or digital knowledge networks:[243] None of them attempt to simulate a closed and meticulously subdivided system, but instead to produce an unfolding cosmos of networking knowledge of individual "plug-ins".[244] The knowledge network created in this way can be entered at any given point and guides the reader on by way of cross-references.[245] The individual parts of the knowledge network can theoretically be supplemented, rejected or replaced by others. Another common feature of all encyclopedic forms of knowledge is the explicit orientation of

235 Diderot and d'Alembert 1751–1780.
236 See Neumann 2004: 123.
237 de Bruyn 2008: 193.
238 Nyiri 2004: 161.
239 Novalis [1799] 1968: 346.
240 Ibid; see Neumann 2004: 125.
241 Neumann 2004: 125.
242 See Luhmann 1981, Gfrereis and Strittmatter 2013.
243 Nyiri 2004: 166–168.
244 Neumann 2004: 125, Latour 2007: 352.
245 Kühn 2009: 162.

its knowledge to praxis, to realization: The quantity of knowledge, regardless of whether it is processed dynamically or statically, should not prevent recognition.[246] The unavoidably sprawling archive should not cloud the desired concentrate of knowledge.[247] All encyclopedic forms of knowledge are linked by the insight that "an unlimited memory capacity" enables "the complete presence of all symbols stored in a culture", and thereby "leads to the destruction of cultural competence".[248] Vast masses of data should thus be archived and classified, but at the same time kept as handy as possible, systematized and liberated from the ballast of false doctrines and superfluous facts.[249]

The encyclopedic knowledge of the late 18th century and Alexander's pattern language are both as heavy as lead and yet as light as a feather, exactly like any elegant theory of practice, in which immense experience is not only accumulated through days of activity and nights of reflection, but is instead synthesized and skillfully sharpened.

In summary, it can be said that Alexander's pattern language orders experiential values in the sense of an encyclopedic science and utilizes them further for purposes of both differentiation and recombination, thus for creative thought. The methodological relationship with Aldo Rossi's almost simultaneously occurring types is obvious at this point: Rossi's types, decoupled from usage and therefore stimulating the imagination, and Alexander's flexible patterns are linked in that they both initiate transformations that are based on experience – not as rigid schemata, but instead as vehicles of creative thought looking "toward new contexts".[250] These "new contexts" are thus also a central theme in Christopher Alexander's work: Building on the thesis of social scientist Herbert Simon, which states that, due to the countless possibilities for solutions, very complex problems cannot be calculated but must instead first be dissected into sub-problems so they can then be recombined into a complete solution with the help of the found sub-solutions, Alexander claims that the actual skill of an architect lies in the ability to judiciously dissect a design problem and cleverly combine the various sub-solutions.[251] Key then is to join together sub-problems and sub-aspects into a

246 de Bruyn 2008: 101.
247 Ibid: 113.
248 Neumann 2004: 138.
249 de Bruyn 2008: 101.
250 Nyiri 2004: 170.
251 Simon 1962, Kühn 2009,
    see Alexander 1964.

"proportional whole"[252] through design. The creative power of the (re)combination of accumulated experience is accordingly not only a central concept of Novalis' encyclopedia, but also a central feature of architectural thought: Because "various stages of development are always present simultaneously when building and combinations of variations are unavoidable",[253] architecture has always been represented as *ars combinatoria* or as *ars recombinatoria*.[254] According to de Bruyn, particularly post-modern concepts like bricolage, montage and collage have reformulated and updated the encyclopedic concept of *ars combinatoria* – like Christopher Alexander's pattern language[255] arising at almost the same time.

Models as tools for re-concretization

Christopher Alexander claims that his patterns represent "timeless" and "natural" forms, which are valid for all people, places and seasons.[256] This statement is perplexing because the designing disciplines in most cases focus on the specificity of the respective situations. The abductively acquired analogies, types and patterns of design may also be generalizations, but they are not "timeless", "natural" or culturally independent forms. The autonomy of each situation and the anchoring of architecture and urban planning in the respective cultural context principally prevent such absolutist reasoning. Especially because designing opens up areas of competence and judgement – thus issues of evaluation, justification and ultimately of morality and ethics – a theory of practice must be conscious of its cultural roots and "ethical function",[257] thus of its fundamentally contingent "phronesis".[258] Consequently, to distinguish it from Alexander's "timeless" and "natural" forms, the goal here is not absolute wisdom or unalterable regularity. Instead, a provisional theory of practice open to subsequent examination and critique should be cultivated that does not cut the cord with complex reality. American urban planner, architect and author Kevin Lynch develops a thought patten that reflects this insight. In his pivotal work entitled *Good City Form*, he therefore distinguishes between theory and model.[259] For him, a theory should include criteria able to

252 Taut [1935/36] 2009: 38, 46–59.
253 de Bruyn 2008: 65.
254 See Shane 2005.
255 de Bruyn 2008: 65.
256 Alexander 1977: xxxv, Kühn 2009: 176.
257 Harries [1985] 2013: 175.
258 See Fleck [1935] 1980.

support models which for their part are already implementable and thus "worthy of emulation".[260] This differentiation ensures theories do not run the risk of being promoted to "natural" rules, because the models bind them to reality like an umbilical cord. Lynch attempts to grasp the criteria of such a theory of practice. To this end, he gathers key performance criteria, which must provide their users with built forms, and differentiates them into five "performance dimensions": vitality, sense, fit, access, control.[261] In his opinion, these are joined by two meta-questions: what is involved with which efforts, and who profits from this to what extent? The cues of these two meta-questions are efficiency and justice. Lynch comes to the conclusion that any theory of practice must also incorporate these 5+2 dimensions linking action and built form into its calculation.[262] Models, on the other hand, are principally already evaluated instructions for implementation, which should be followed in the sense of a practical "prototype".[263] Models connect theories to reality. Following this notion of differentiating between theory and model, the five points of Le Corbusier can be identified more precisely as five parts of a model, or even as five models, of his more general theory of modernity. According to Lynch, both models and theories are necessary. The former, because complex, real problems in a limited time frame are simply not manageable without models as prototypes; and the latter, because the creation of models is not possible without syntheses of merged and ordered practical knowledge, experiential knowledge and knowledge of principles.[264] It is conspicuous that this reasoning is closely related to Schinkel's aforementioned principle of "realization" and could probably be considered the simplest response to a desire for absence of theory. Under the heading "Models as Possibilities"[265] Lynch proposes a collection of non-neutral models – evaluated through judgement and perceived as implementable – as "holistic patterns" for various situations.[266] This proposition is highly reminiscent of Schinkel's, who had no general theory in mind for the plans for his (unfortunately never realized) work *Das Architektonische Lehrbuch*[267] [The Architectural Textbook], but instead a dynamic and flexible collection of "suitable examples"

259 Lynch 1981: 285.
260 Ibid: 277.
261 Ibid: 111, see Illies 2008.
262 Lynch 1981: 111–118
263 Ibid: 277.
264 Ibid: 288.
265 Ibid: 289.
266 See Flyvbjerg 2001: 20.
267 Schinkel, in Peschken 1979: 34.

reacting to each new construction task. Schinkel was very aware that the formulation of "the most complete possible series of such examples" strived for represents an endless encyclopedic task. According to Lynch, models must be explicitly evaluated and justified in order to apply as "suitable examples". These are not yet the individual components of the experience repertoire.

After determining that no such collection of models yet existed, Lynch endeavors to sketch a model that transfers individual descriptions of properties and experiential values into a viable and implementable synthesis that is thus "worthy of emulation": The "alternating net".[268] (Figure 12)

Figure 12.
The alternating net model (Lynch 1981)

After describing the model, that he calls an "alternating net", Lynch lists the performative properties of this model he had previously demanded:

This [...] model refers at once to map pattern, flow pattern, the grain of use and density, the distribution of control, and a cyclical pattern of change and how it is implemented. Presumably, these elements are fitted one to another. The motives are adaptability [...] and good generalized access, combined with a high degree of access to open space and a sharp grain of local access, as well as a wide variety of density and activity and a diversity of modal choice. An efficient means of central control is allied to a convenient way of escaping that central control. The model produces three widely different yet connected habitats (the arterial frontage, the "slow" frontage, and the rural interior), and a strong sense of time, via the cycling of the grids and the retention of the permanent symbolic locations.[269]

268 Lynch 1981: 286–287.
269 Ibid: 288.

Elsewhere in his text, Lynch refers to the meta-properties upon which his preferred models would be based:
The reader will see that [...] general preferences – development, within continuity, via openness and connection – underlie all the succeeding pages, even while the theory makes an effort to see that it is applicable to any context. [...] The bias of the teacher is now unmasked. [...] There is an inherent tension as well as a circularity between continuity and development – between the stabilities and connections needed for coherence and the ability to change and grow (equals openness).[270]

Concluding the presentation of his model Lynch observes:
Speculative as it is, and vulnerable to criticism (as it should be), it serves to illustrate what is meant by a model that deals with form, process, and management all working together.[271]

By way of ordering knowledge (theory) and ethical deliberations (judgement) the processed repertoires of experience can be transferred into a new stage: as models, they are now considered worthy of emulation, "prototypes", referring to one another in terms of form, process and management.[272] Models make complex, real problems manageable in a limited timeframe, and thus function as open tools of realization. Open because the justification patterns of a model become visible and criticizable[273] thus enabling critique and connection for other patterns of justification, theories and models. In order to achieve the utmost goal of a theory of practice, the ordered knowledge can be emulated in practice as a justified and substantial cultural concept in the form of conclusive syntheses – or according to Lynch as models – and thus substantially enrich the manifestness, performativity, reflexivity and measuredness of the realization.

Interestingly, it now becomes apparent that models are not rules, but instead conclusive syntheses. Another term for such conclusive syntheses are Flyvbjerg's "holistic patterns" mentioned at the beginning of this work. These "holistic patterns" were introduced as the basis of the intuitive, "virtuosic" action,

270 Ibid: 117.
271 Ibid: 288.
272 Ibid: 276.
273 Boltanski and Thévenot [1991] 2007: 289, 303–311.

which help structure each new situation.[274] However, these same "holistic patterns" are now no longer merely random ideas or flashes of insight, but instead products of the ordering dimension of design. As models or prototypes, they re-enter the design process. The circle closes: the "holistic patterns" that feed design can be designed via the detour of experience, the power of judgement and of theory by the designers themselves!

This loop that brings the ordering dimension of design back into the design action by way of models is another iteration form of design. In conclusion we can state that the pattern of thought of a "theory of practice" feeds on reality and, with the help of design, experience and power of judgement, creates "holistic patterns" to in turn be able to fertilize the design aspired to. (Fig. 13) The direction of knowledge creation from reality to theory is mainly abductive and inductive (Fig. 13, top arrow) and its objective is sound realization. (Figure 13, lower arrow)

---

274 Flyvbjerg 2001: 20.

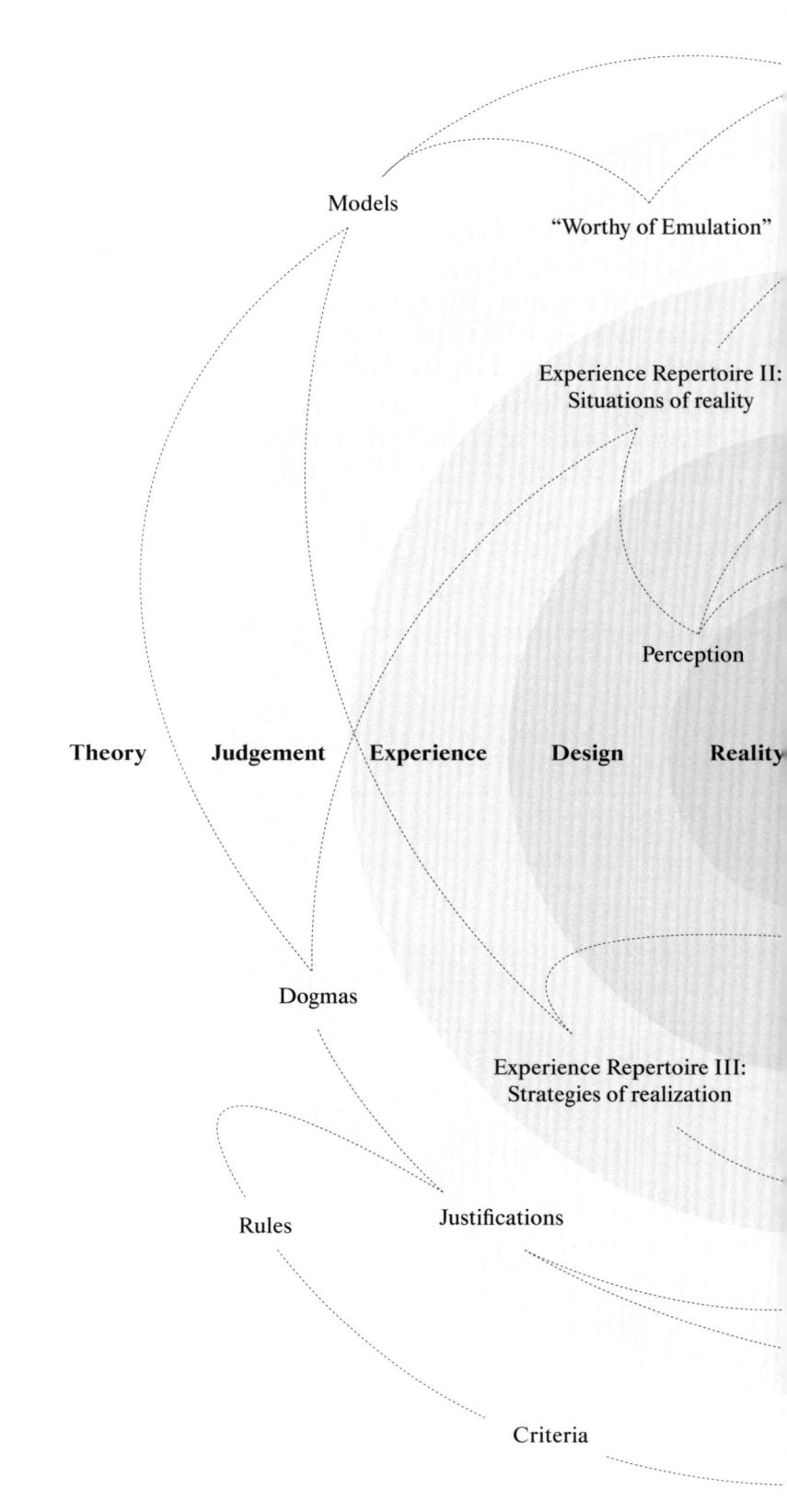

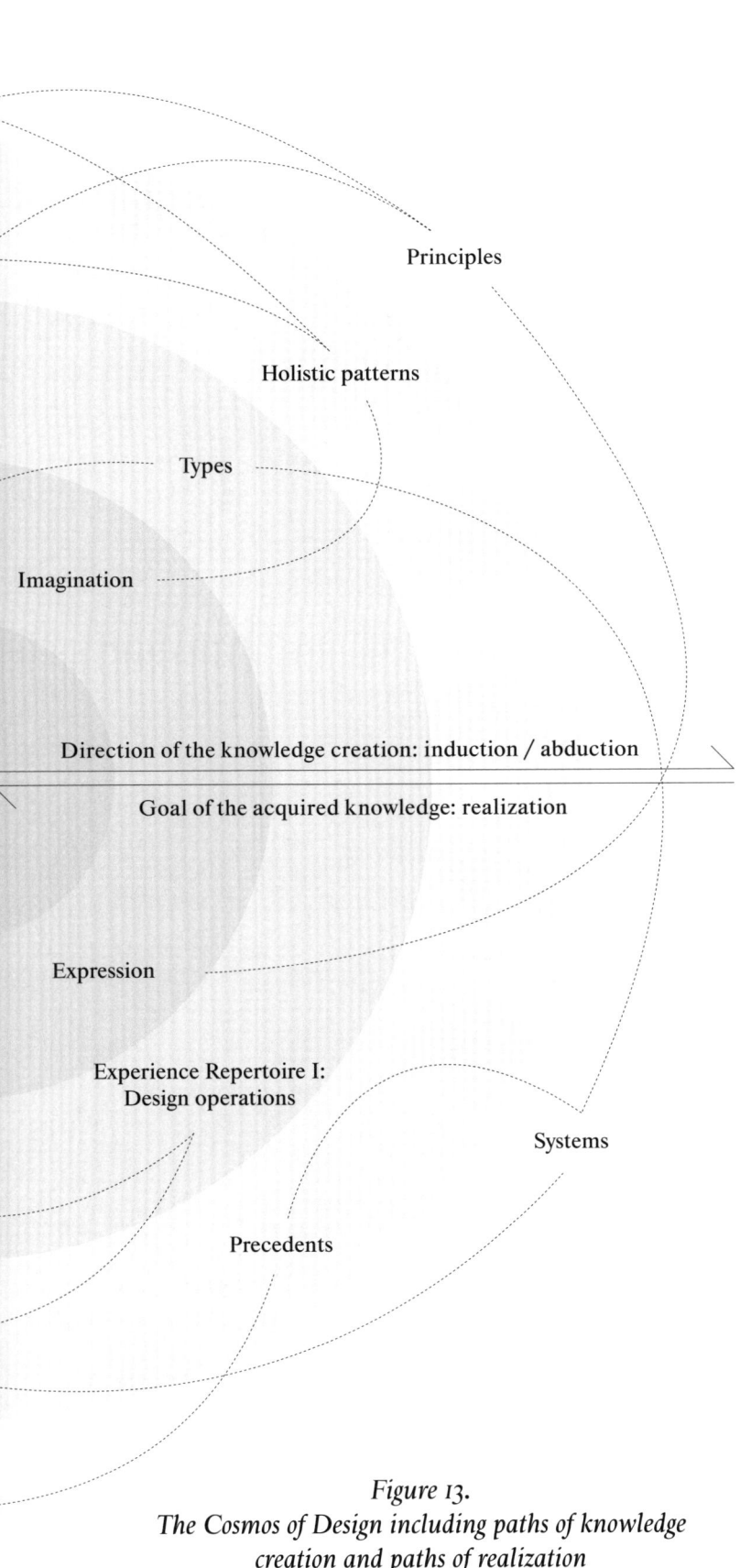

Figure 13.
The Cosmos of Design including paths of knowledge creation and paths of realization

Synopsis:
The Cosmos of Design

The specific iteration form of design

After another loop of design having been completed in the last chapter, namely that of the ordering dimension, all three dimensions of design are now represented: the changing dimension, the examining dimension and the ordering dimension. Each of the three dimensions demonstrates a different form of iteration. Together, they form the *specific iteration form of design*. (Figure 14)

The specific iteration form is initiated by design as a primary action. (Fig. 14, part A) Design thus becomes the core and the initial operation. Flowing from this primary action into the three dimensions are the impulses (Fig. 14, part B), which each meet with reality in a specific form. They subsequently return, saturated with experience, into the design action, in order to repeat it in an improved fashion thanks to new insight. (Fig. 14, part C) This return involves an iterative re-entry into the design form.[275] The primary action of design, which is constantly repeated, holds the three iteration types together. It is its source and its outlet. The three iteration types that arise from the primary action are summarized in the following.

The first iteration type originates from the changing dimension of design, where iteration loops optimize the projects for the improvement of reality. (Fig. 14, part D) The iteration type of the changing dimension also creates images, texts, plans and concepts as to how reality might be changed in the concrete case. In the process, these documents change "the idea" of a design as defined by Schön, which can then be used and tested in a new iteration loop. (Figure 14, part E) This iteration type is very direct. If what is designed does not yet correspond with the inner ideal, an additional design loop is required. This is an "iteration of optimization" regarding an approximation of the inner image to the designed project. The designed project is evaluated in this context in keeping with its potential for transforming reality, and this not in a general sense, but rather in the respective specific case.

The iteration type of the examining dimension attempts to understand and illuminate reality, always with the goal of

275 See Spencer-Brown 1969.

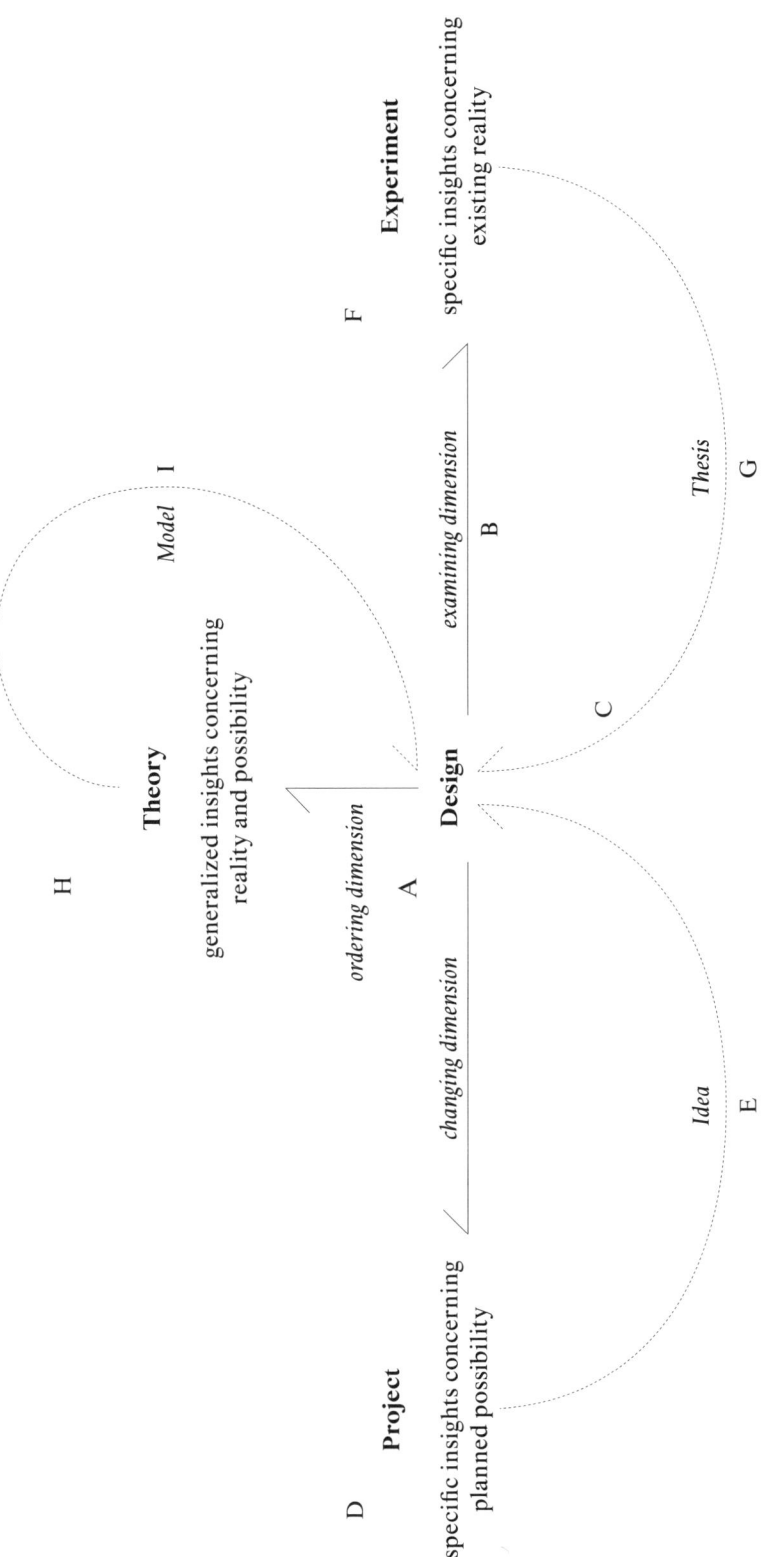

Figure 14.
The specific iteration form of design

subsequently also being able to change it for the better. It describes how design not only changes reality, but also how the designing experiment examines reality. (Fig. 14, part F) In the process, new perspectives of reality are initially created protoabductively. The insights following from this can then be converted into theses that subject reality to a speculative logic in Ungers' sense and thus "rationalize the existing". Correspondingly, insights concerning the existing reality are created. The result is a new thesis with regard to reality. (Fig. 14, part G) The evaluation of design as an experiment takes place in accordance with its potential for transformatively examining reality. As presented in the section on abduction, such theses serve not only the purpose of further illumination, but instead also stimulate design. This is because they change the perspective on reality, meaning that wishes for change, design ideas and strategies are also conceived of anew. In this way, the examining dimension of design also provokes a new design loop.

The iteration type of the ordering dimension spans a variety of design operations and develops over an extended period. This iteration type arises from various individual iterations and thus represents a type of "iteration of a higher order". Presented in the previous section it states that design nurtures experience and judgement, which in turn produce ordered knowledge, thus theory. (Fig. 14, part H) In the process, insights on both the possible change and the interpretation of reality are linked. These insights can then be synthesized in models worthy of implementation, which transcend reality both across cases and in an abstracting fashion. (Fig. 14, part I) Such models are ethically reflected upon overall concepts for positively changing reality. Their evaluation takes place in accordance with their potential for transcending reality, and in accordance with their potential for realizing ethical and aesthetic concepts.[276] The re-entry into design for this iteration type takes place in Lynch's sense as concepts, prototypes and models. They too provoke new design loops.

The three iteration forms are not independent of one another. Quite the opposite. Because they are in fact three dimensions of the central design action, they constantly inform and

[276] See Spector 2001.

influence one another when designing. They thus point out the path back to the central pattern of thought of the examination. This states that design can be conceived of as the indivisible core and initial operation of three different dimensions: Design as a projective instrument for changing reality, design as an examining means for acquiring knowledge and design as the resource of a structuring theory of practice. In the process, realization, the acquiring of knowledge and the formation of theories are conceived of as three directions or dimensions of one and the same designing primary action.

The Cosmos of Design: an overview

Following a long journey through the processes of thought and paths of reflection of design, a summarizing overview with all three dimensions and their iteration loops of design can be ventured in order to complete the arc with the core thesis of this work. (Figure 15)

The figure is briefly introduced below: starting from the design action, the changing dimension and the examining dimension can be differentiated. These two dimensions are based on the conception propounded by Schön and originate from the central design operation, which in turn arises out of reality and at the same time changes and illuminates it. The project changes reality, applies ideas, tests them and generates new ideas. The experiment examines reality in an explanatory fashion based on theses (Fig. 15, left half). Three experience products arise from the repeated application of this iteration loop: Repertoire I of the design operations, Repertoire II of strategies, which arises from the changing dimension, and Repertoire III of situations, which arise from the examining dimension (Fig. 15, center). Through experiential knowledge, which is theoretically sharpened by means of judgement and theory and ethically evaluated, thus via the ordering dimension, the acquired, encyclopedic knowledge finds its way back into reality in the form of "holistic patterns" and evaluated models as experiential values. (Fig. 15, right half) The direction of the knowledge creation here is mainly abductive

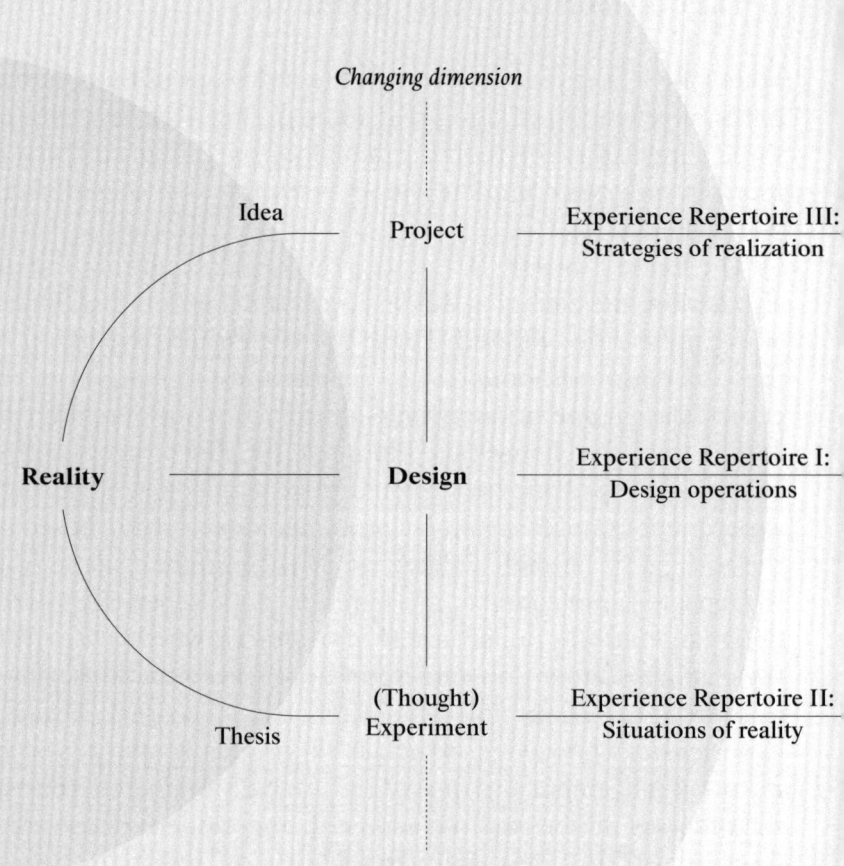

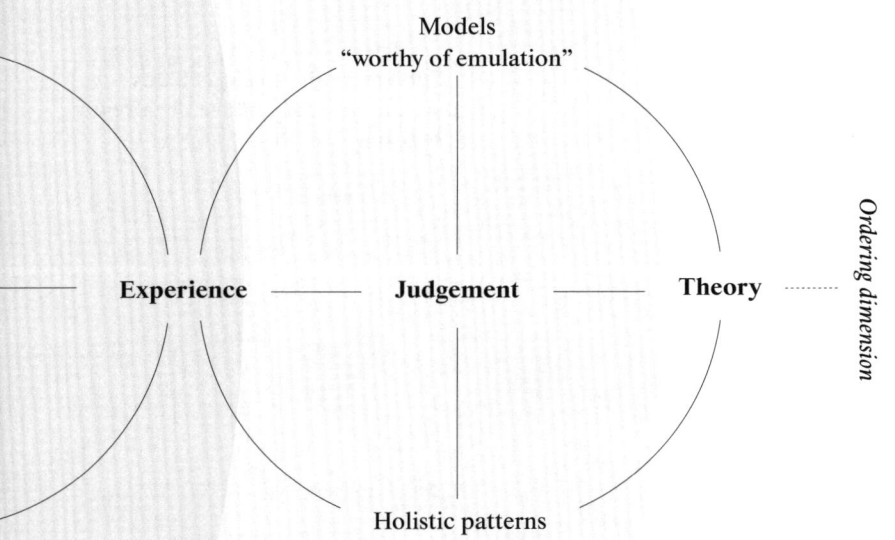

Figure 15.
The Cosmos of Design
Relationships of the changing, examining and ordering dimensions of design.

The changing dimension of design

Design is an action that represents a potential change of reality in space and time. Potentials are attributions of possibility in specific contextual networks. The design is the tool that makes this potential for change visible.

    Project
Design (im)possible futures

    Idea
Imagination or mental concept of a possible change or solution

The examining dimension of design

Design is an action that transformatively examines realities and correspondingly allows them to be perceived as changed. In the process, not only an operation is tested on the respective reality, but also reality on the operation. Consequently, the design can be an experiment that promotes insight, in the course of which the qualities and conditions of a reality are examined.

    (Thought) Experiment
Examine reality in a way that changes it

    Thesis
Subject reality to a speculative thesis and thus rationalize the already existing

Repertoires as experience products of design

Experience finds its way into the repertoires of the designer in the form of holistic patterns. As analogies, they can be compared with each new situation for similarity and difference and adapted further. The repertoires are, so to speak, the storehouse of experience that can be accessed when designing. They should be understood as a fund, which is applied to the respective newly occurring situation in the form of types, analogies, metaphors, images and ideas. Three repertoire categories can be differentiated.

   Experience Repertoire I:
   Design operations
Tools of targeted irritation achieved through design itself

   Experience Repertoire II:
   Situations of reality
Types of reality achieved through the examining dimension of design

   Experience Repertoire III:
   Strategies of realization
Paths of realization achieved through the changing dimension of design

The ordering dimension of design

The acquired, encyclopedic knowledge finds its way back into reality and directly into the design action by way of ordered and evaluated experiential knowledge, thus by way of the theoretical dimension of design in the form of holistic patterns and evaluated models.

   Experience
Practical knowledge across cases, upon which new design operations are based

   Judgement
Transfer of the experiential values into a criticizable stage

   Theory
Product of an open synthesis procedure of experience processing, which generates ordered knowledge and accompanies design practice in a structuring fashion

   Holistic patterns
Evaluated types of social-spatial constellations that serve in unknown situations as comparisons when looking for similarity and difference

   Evaluated models
Ethically reflected and applicable prototypes for implementation; "worthy of emulation" according to Kevin Lynch

Legend for Figure 15.
The Cosmos of Design
Relationships of the changing, examining
and ordering dimensions of design.

and inductive. (Fig. 15, top arrow) Its goal is sound realization. (Fig. 15, lower arrow) The constellations of this multitude of relationships span the *Cosmos of Design*, which every designer or design team wanders through iteratively on many different paths again and again, consciously and unconsciously, and further illuminates when designing.

The performativity of the Cosmos of Design

The *Cosmos of Design* developed and presented in this book is not a set of instructions for design, but instead a systematic representation of cognitive and thought processes of design. It is an explanatory model and could also have been titled "The Rationalization of Design" in Ungers' sense or "The Architecture of Design" in keeping with Rossi.

This inevitably raises the question of whom and how this account of the thought processes of design can help (further). Key here is that just like design itself, the performativity of the *Cosmos of Design* also has many faces. These are highlighted below. First, the contributions inherent to the subject for the explicitly designing disciplines will be presented, followed by the interdisciplinary points of contact and insights.

Let us start with the contributions inherent to the design subject: The *Cosmos of Design* should not be understood as a method within disciplines. Like in the section concerning design as qualitative-heuristic experimentation in Chapter 2, this would also be unrewarding given the methodological openness of design. Rather, the systematic representation should first improve the understanding of design, second, theoretically order the insights acquired from this and, third, accompany design practice in a guiding fashion. The form of the accompaniment can on the one hand be understood metaphorically as a map, which can be used in the confusing terrain of design, with all of its loops and interfaces, to find out where one is and what one is doing at the moment. It helps to improve the localization and contextualization in the thought terrain of design. On the other hand, the specific descriptions of abduction and of iteration help to comprehend and better deploy those thought processes, which mostly take place unconsciously while designing. In the process, the intuitive, random and imaginative sides of design should under no circumstances be abolished in the name of a banal interpretation of enlightenment, but should instead be appreciated and productively employed in the sense of reflexive enlightenment.[277] Ideally, the *Cosmos of Design* should help designers to intellectually and emotionally access their activity, to thus also deploy it self-confidently and not least to enjoy it and continue discovering. An overview is said to create new freedoms, and these in turn provide impulses for adventurous curiosity. So much for the subject of didactic value, which can be especially useful in design teaching or when reflecting upon one's own practical activity.

The *Cosmos of Design* also demonstrates that design practice, design theory and the use of design in research collectives not only stratifies and specializes but should primarily be held together by the basal action of design. Design is accordingly conceived of as an integral form of thought. The central pattern of thought of the examination should thus show that design can be conceived of as the source and outlet of three different dimensions. In this process, realization, the acquiring of knowledge and the formation of theories are conceived of as three directions or dimensions of one and the same designing primary action. From this primary action, impulses flow along the three dimensions, which then meet with reality and subsequently return, saturated with experience, to the design action, in order to repeat it in an improved fashion. As soon as these three dimensions are separated or isolated from one another, they are no longer capable of contributing to the changing of reality (through design). A schism within disciplines would accordingly have serious consequences. A central composition of the *Cosmos of Design* is thus the justification of this primary action with its three dimensions.

This work, together with its justification, can also contribute to the creation of a design curriculum. It can be used as the foundation for design training conceived from design itself,

---

[277] Accordingly, this work is located within the Romantic tradition, which extended the project of the Enlightenment to the interior of the human condition, without attempting to do away with its wondrous sides. (see Lyotard 1979, Safranski 2007, Salewski 2012).

especially through its broadly conceived concept of design, which contains not only the central aspects of design, but also its peripheral aspects and interfaces with other epistemological, artistic and practical disciplines in particular. In contrast with approaches that establish curricula through the accumulation of disciplines, which one should also occupy oneself with as a designer or a design team (for example, sociology, mathematics or ecology), the *Cosmos of Design* focuses on the action and reflection of design (for example, the formation of patterns through experience, the rationalization of the existing through design or the protoabduction through experiments). The two approaches – on the one hand the structuring of the discipline inherent to design and the understanding of the inner logic of design, and on the other, the accumulation of those disciplines that are also of relevance for the design discipline – are not mutually exclusive, but could instead form the basis for a design curriculum as complementary approaches. Contemporary curricula of architecture and design schools tend to rely to a great extent on the accumulation of disciplines. A logic inherent to design may be used for the structure of design courses, but seldom for a higher-level conception of design training. This also because design is all too often degraded to a discipline and is not understood as a form of thought that must be more broadly comprehended and that is also transdisciplinary in nature.

From an inter- and transdisciplinary perspective, this work should provide those in research teams occupied with the inherent logic of design with insights into the functionality of design thought processes. Design should thus make a less erratic impression and should therefore neither be mystified nor unnecessarily side-lined. Appropriation begins with curious empathy, and it is precisely this that the *Cosmos of Design* should arouse. This work therefore offers several points of contact, namely the concepts of abduction, typification, experimental thought and heuristics. This is most clearly apparent in the section on the specific form of abduction of design, in which abduction is designated as an interface and crossing between Peirce's cognitive triad and the design triad presented in this book. Not only "episteme" and "praxis" intersect at this point, but also heuristics and empiricism. The transdisciplinary aspect of this is not the striving for identical methods or the transfer of the methods of one discipline to another,[278] but instead the linking of various forms of thought into a more comprehensive project for the production of insights, as is shown with the pattern of thought of the *double loop of knowledge creation*. In this context, the work should help to clarify the role of design in the edifice of science and thus prepare it for transdisciplinary projects. It is thereby important to emphasize that design is neither "epistemologized" nor broken down into its individual parts (art, theory and research). Although these two approaches are tempting and are therefore often attempted, they are not appropriate for the essence of design. The point is instead to understand the deeper forms of thought, such as heuristics and empiricism, including their roles, and to marry them with other dimensions. Consequently, this work is to be seen as a contribution to a foundation for science, which first understands practice, theory and research as interrelated and mutually dependent, and secondly as heuristic and empirical aspects. In this way, an expanded picture of cognitive production should be co-founded, which not only allows for various disciplines and focuses of thought, but which also embeds these into a holistic project of knowledge creation. This project cultivates differences, places them in a mutual relationship and does not deliver them unto far-reaching and especially insurmountable schisms. In the process, holistic models of explanation should be prepared for our structures of meaning and made accessible for a conceptualization of reality that combines perspectives. The goal is a kind of meta-discipline of the creation and application of knowledge.[279] As is shown in this book, design and its cognitive potential play a decisive role in the process.

---

278 See Latour 2007 for the representation of such a momentous experiment.
279 See Bateson 1982, Wilson 1998.

Bibliography &
List of illustrations

Aicher, O. (1991): analog und digital. Berlin: Ernst & Sohn.
Alberti, L. B. ([approx. 1443-1452] 1485): De re aedificatoria libri decem. Florence: Alamanus.
Albrechts, L. (2004): Strategic (Spatial) Planning Reexamined. In: Environment and Planning B: Planning and Design, 31. 743-758.
Alexander, C. (1971): The state of the art in design methods. In: DMG Newsletter 5 (3). 1-7.
Alexander, C.; Ishikawa, S.; Silverstein, M. (1977): A Pattern Language. New York: Oxford University.
Ammon, S. (2015): Perpektiven architekturphilosophischer Entwurfsforschung. In: Gleiter, J; Schwarte, L. (Eds.): Architektur und Philosophie. Bielefeld: transcript.
Aristotle ([335 B.C.] 1976): The Nicomachean Ethics. Harmondsworth: Penguin.
Balsiger, P. (2005): Transdisziplinarität. Systematisch-vergleichende Untersuchung disziplinübergreifender Wissenschaftspraxis. Munich/Paderborn: Fink.
Baumberger, C. (Ed. 2013): Architekturphilosophie. Grundlagentexte. Münster: Mentis.
Bateson, G. (1982): Geist und Natur. Eine notwendige Einheit. Frankfurt: Suhrkamp.
Bayazit, N. (2004): Investigating Design: A Review of Forty Years of Design Research. In: Design Issues, 20 (1). 16-29.
Bideau, A. (2011): Architektur und symbolisches Kapital. Bilderzählungen und Identitätsproduktion bei O.M. Ungers. Basel: Birkhäuser.
Blaser, W. (1977): Mies van der Rohe. Lehre und Schule / Principles and School. Basel: Birkhäuser.
Blumenberg, H. (2006): Arbeit am Mythos. Frankfurt: Suhrkamp.
Boltanski, L.; Thévenot, L. ([1991] 2007): Über die Rechtfertigung. Hamburg: Edition.
Bolzano, B. (1837): Erfindungskunst. In: Ibid: Versuch einer ausführlichen und größtentheils neuen Darstellung der Logik mit steter Rücksicht auf deren bisherige Bearbeiter. Third volume. Sulzbach: Seidel. 293-303.
Boucsein, B. (2014): Situationen. Vom Sehen, Erleben und Verändern städtischer Räume. In: Professor Kees Christiaanse; Rieniets, T.; Kretschmann, N.; Perret, M.: Die Stadt als Ressource. Berlin: Jovis. 25-35.
Bourdieu, P. (1972): Esquisse d'une théorie de la pratique, précédé de trois études d'ethnologie kabyle. Geneva: Droz.
Broadbent, G. (1979): The development of design methods. Design Methods and Theories 13(1), 41-45.

Burckhardt, L. ([1980] 2012): Design ist unsichtbar. Entwurf, Gesellschaft & Pädagogik. Berlin: Martin Schmitz.
Cepl, J. (2007): Oswald Mathias Ungers. Eine intellektuelle Biografie. Cologne: Verlag der Buchhandlung Walther König.
Cassirer, E. ([1925] 1994): Philosophie der symbolischen Formen. Volume II: Das Mythische Denken. Darmstadt: Wissenschaftliche Buchgesellschaft.
Christensen, K. S. (1985): Coping with uncertainty in planning. In: Journal of the American Planning Association. Vol. 51/1. 63-73.
Christiaanse, K.; Van den Born, H.; Van Oort, I. (2005, Eds.): Situation. KCAP Architects and Planners. Basel/Boston: Birkhäuser.
Creuzer, F.; Daub, K. (Eds. 1805): Studien. Volume I. Frankfurt and Heidelberg: J. C. B. Mohr.
Cross, N. (Ed. 1984): Developments in Design Methodology, Chichester, UK: John Wiley & Sons Ltd.
Cross, N. (2006): Designerly ways of knowing. London: Springer.
Damasio, A. (1994): Descartes' Error. Emotion, Reason and the Human Brain. New York: Putnam.
Damasio, A. (1999): The Feeling of What Happens. Body and Emotion in the Making of Consciousness. New York: Harcourt Brace.
Damasio, A. (2010): Self Comes to Mind: Constructing the Conscious Brain. New York: Pantheon.
deBono, E. (1970): Lateral Thinking. A Textbook of Creativity. London: Penguin.
Delaney, C.F. (1993): Science, Knowledge and Mind: A Study in the Philosophy of C. S. Peirce. Indiana: Notre Dame.
de Bruyn, G. (2008): Die enzyklopädische Architektur. Bielefeld: transcript.
Dewey, J. (1903): Studies in Logical Theory. Chicago: University of Chicago Press.
Dewey, J. (1910): How we think: A restatement of the relation of reflective thinking to the educative process. Boston: DC Heath.
Dewey, J. (1925): Experience and Nature. Chicago: Open Court Publishing.
Dewey, J. (1927b): The Role of Philosophy in the History of Civilization. In: Philosophical Review 36 (1). 1-9.
Dewey, J. (1929): The Quest for Certainty: a study of the relation of knowledge and action. New York: Minton Balch.
Dewey, J. (1934): Art as Experience. New York: Minton Balch.
Dewey, J. ([1938] 2002): Logik. Die Theorie der Forschung. Frankfurt: Suhrkamp.
Dewey, J. ([1938] 1997): Experience and Education. New York: Touchstone.

Diderot, M.; d'Alembert, M. (1751–1780): Encyclopédie ou Dictionnaire raisonné des sciences, des arts et des métiers. Paris: Academie Royale des Sciences de Paris.
Dörner, D. (1974): Die kognitive Organisation beim Problemlösen. Versuche einer kybernetischen Theorie der elementaren Informationsverarbeitungsprozesse beim Denken. Bern: Huber.
Dörner, D. (2001): Die Logik des Misslingens. Reinbek: Rowohlt.
Dorst, K. (2003): Understanding Design. 150 Reflections on Being a Designer. Amsterdam: BIS.
Dreyfus, H.; Dreyfus, S. (1988): Mind over Machine: The Power of Human Intuition and Expertise in the Era of the Computer. New York: Free Press.
Ebert, T. (1995): Phronêsis. Anmerkungen zu einem Begriff der Aristotelischen Ethik (VI 5, 8–13). In: Höffe, O. (Ed.): Aristoteles. Die Nikomachische Ethik. Berlin: Akademie. 165-185.
Einstein, A. (1916): Über die spezielle und allgemeine Relativitätstheorie (gemeinverständlich). Braunschweig: Vieweg.
Einstein, A. (1973): Ideas and Opinions. New York: Dell.
Eisenman, P. ([1963] 2006): The Formal Basis of Modern Architecture. Zurich: Lars Müller.
Eisenman, P. (1982): The Houses of Memory: The Texts of Analogy. In: Rossi, A.: The Architecture of the City. Cambridge, Mass.: MIT Press.
Eisenman, P. (1987): Houses of Cards. New York: Oxford University Press.
Eisenman, P. (2005): Ins Leere geschrieben. Schriften & Interviews 2. Vienna: Passagen.
Eisenman, P. (2008): Ten Canonical Buildings 1950–2000 New York: Rizzoli International.
Eisinger, A. (2008): Stop Making Sense. In: Swiss Federal Office of Culture: Explorations in Architecture. Teaching, Design, Research. 14–33.
Faste, T.; Faste, H. (2012): Demystifying "Design Research": Design is Not Research, Research is Design. IDSA Education Symposium.
Feger, H. (1985): Ressourcentheorie sozialer Beziehungen. In: Albert, D. (Ed.): Bericht über den 34. Kongreß der Deutschen Gesellschaft für Psychologie, Vol. I. Göttingen: Hogrefe. 480–482.
Feierabend, P. (1976): Wider den Methodenzwang. Skizze einer Anarchistischen Erkenntnistheorie. Frankfurt: Suhrkamp.

Fezer, J. (2009): A Non-Sentimental Argument. Die Krisen des Design Methode Movement 1962–1972. In: Gethmann, D.; Hauser, S. (Eds.): Kulturtechnik Entwerfen. Praktiken, Konzepte und Medien in Architektur und Design Science. Bielefeld: transcript. 287–304.
Fischer, G. (1999): Vitruv NEU oder Was ist Architektur? Basel: Birkhäuser.
Fleck, L. ([1935] 1980): Entstehung und Entwicklung einer wissenschaftlichen Tatsache: Einführung in die Lehre vom Denkstil und Denkkollektiv. Frankfurt: Suhrkamp.
Flyvbjerg, B. (1998): Rationality and Power: Democracy in Practice. Chicago: University of Chicago Press.
Flyvbjerg, B. (2001): Making Social Science Matter. Why social inquiry fails and how it can succeed again. Cambridge: Cambridge University Press.
Forester, J. (1989): Planning in the Face of Power. Berkeley: University of California.
Forester, J. (2009): Dealing with Differences: Dramas of Mediating Public Disputes. Oxford: Oxford University Press.
Galen, C. ([approx. 200] 1528): Claudii Galeni Pergameni Definitiones medicae, Iona Philologo interprete. Paris: Colines.
Gänshirt, C. (2011): Werkzeuge für Ideen. Eine Einführung ins architektonische Entwerfen. Basel: Birkhäuser.
Gedenryd, H. (1998): How designers work. Lund: Lund University.
Giedion, S. ([1941] 1965): Raum, Zeit, Architektur. Die Entstehung einer neuen Tradition. Ravensburg: Maier.
Gleiter, J. H. (2008): Architekturtheorie heute. Bielefeld: transcript.
Gleiter, J. H.; Schwarte, L. (Eds. 2015): Architektur und Philosophie. Bielefeld: transcript.
Gleiter, J. H. (2017): Vom Abreißen der Modellierungskette. Entwerfen im digitalen Zeitalter. In: Ammon, S.; Hinterwalder, I. (Eds.) Bildlichkeit im Zeitalter der Modellierung. Operative Artefakte in Entwurfsprozessen der Architektur und des Ingenieurwesens. Paderborn: Fink. 91-103.
Gfrereis, H.; Strittmatter, E. (Eds. 2013): Zettelkästen. Maschinen der Phantasie. Ausstellungskatalog. Marbach a. N.: Deutsche Schillergesellschaft.
Halbwachs, M. ([1939] 1950): La mémoire collective. Paris: PUF.
Haldane, J. (1999): Form, Meaning and Value. A History of the Philosophy of Architecture. In: The Journal of Architecture, 4. 9–20.
Hartkopf, W.; Baum, H.; Hengst, M.; Schmid-Kowarzik, W. (1987): Dialektik – Heurisik – Logik. Nachgelassene Studien. Bodenheim: Athenaeum.

Healey, P. (2009a): In Search of the 'Strategic' in Spatial Strategy Making. In: Planning Theory & Practice 10, No. 4. 439-57.

Healey, P. (2009b): The pragmatic tradition in planning thought. In: Journal of Planning Education and Research 28 (3). 277-292.

Harries, K. ([1985] 2013): Die ethische Funktion der Architektur. In: Baumberger, C (Ed.): Architekturphilosophie. Grundlagentexte. Münster: mentis. 167-179.

Heidegger, M. ([1927] 2001): Sein und Zeit. Max Niemeyer Verlag. Tübingen Niemeyer.

Hertzberger, H. (1976): Strukturalismus – Ideologie. In: Bauen + Wohnen 1/76. 21-24.

Hoch, C. (2007): Pragmatic communicative action theory. In: Journal of Planning Education and Research 26 (3). 272-283.

Illies, C. (2008): The Moral Relevance of Architecture. In: IAPS Bulletin. 3-6.

Illies, C.; Ray, N. (2014): Philosophy of Architecture. Cambridge: Cambridge Architectural Press.

Jaspers, K. ([1923] 1980): Die Idee der Universität. Heidelberg/Berlin/New York: Springer.

Johannes, R. (Ed. 2009): Entwerfen. Architektenausbildung in Europa von Vitruv bis Mitte des 20. Jahrhunderts. Geschichte – Theorie – Praxis. Hamburg: Junius.

Johnson, M. (1987): The Body in the Mind. The Bodily Basis of Meaning, Imagination, and Reason. Chicago: University Press.

Jones, J.; Thornley, D. (Eds. 1963): Conference on Design Methods. Oxford, UK: Pergamon Press.

Kant, I. (1781): Kritik der reinen Vernunft. Riga: Hartknoch.

Kant, I. ([1790] 1974): Kritik der Urteilskraft. Frankfurt: Suhrkamp.

Kleining, G. ([1982] 1994): Umriss zu einer Methodologie qualitativer Sozialforschung. In: Ibid: Qualitativ-heuristische Sozialforschung, Hamburg: Fechner. 12-46.

Kleining, G. ([1986] 1994): Das qualitative Experiment. In: Ibid: Qualitativ-heuristische Sozialforschung, Hamburg: Fechner. 148-177.

Klüsener, S. (1998): Qualitative Heuristik. Strukturierendes Entdecken. Heidelberg: Ruprecht-Karls-Universität.

Kolb, D. A. (1984): Experimental Learning. Englewood Cliffs NJ: Prentice Hall.

Konersmann, R. (2006): Kulturelle Tatsachen. Frankfurt: Suhrkamp.

Koolhaas, R. (1978): Delirious New York. A Retroactive Manifesto for Manhattan. London: Thames and Hudson.

Kollhoff, H. (2018): Von der Stadt zur Fassade. Interview with Hans Kollhoff, Berlin-Mitte, 05/16/2018. In: Fink, L.; Fink, T.; Bernegger, R. (Eds.): Berliner Portraits. Erzählungen zur Architektur der Stadt. Cologne: Verlag der Buchhandlung Walther König. 159-178.

Kretz, S.; Salewski, C. (2014): Urbanität der Dinge. In: Professor Kees Christiaanse; Rieniets, T.; Kretschmann, N.; Perret, M.: Die Stadt als Ressource. Berlin: Jovis. 167-180.

Kühn, C. (2009): Erste Schritte zu einer Theorie des Ganzen. Christopher Alexander und die "Notes on the Synthesis of Form." In: Gethmann, D.; Hauser, S. (Eds.) Kulturtechnik Entwerfen. Praktiken, Konzepte und Medien in Architektur und Design Science. Bielefeld: transcript.

Kühne, U. (2005): Die Methode des Gedankenexperiments. Frankfurt: Suhrkamp.

Lagueux, M. (2004): Ethics versus Aesthetics in Architecture. In: The Philosophical Forum 35. 117-133.

Latour, B. (2007): Eine neue Soziologie für eine neue Gesellschaft. Einführung in die Akteur-Netzwerk-Theorie Frankfurt: Suhrkamp.

Laurel, B. (Ed. 2003): Design Research: Methods and Perspectives. Cambridge, Mass.: MIT Press.

Lawson, B. (1980): How Designers Think. The Design Process Demystified. Oxford: Architectural Press.

Lawson, B. (1994): Design in Mind. Oxford: Butterworth-Heinemann.

Lawson, B. (2004): What Designers Know. Oxford: Architectural Press.

Lawson, B.; Dorst, C. (2009): Design Expertise. Oxford: Architectural Press.

Le Corbusier; Jeanneret, P. ([1923] 1927): Fünf Punkte zu einer neuen Architektur. In: Die Form. Zeitschrift für gestaltende Arbeit. No. 2. 272-274.

Lenk, H. (2000): Kreative Aufstiege. Zur Philosophie und Psychologie der Kreativität. Frankfurt: Suhrkamp.

Lévy-Strauss, C. (1962): Le Pensée sauvage. Paris: Pocket.

List, E. (2009): Die Kreativität des Lebendigen und die Entstehung des Neuen. In: Gethmann, D.; Hauser, S. (Eds.): Kulturtechnik Entwerfen. Praktiken, Konzepte und Medien in Architektur und Design Science. Bielefeld: transcript. 319-332.

Luhmann, N. (1981): Kommunikation mit Zettelkästen. Ein Erfahrungsbericht. In: Baier, H. et al.: Öffentliche Meinung und sozialer Wandel. Opladen: Westdeutscher Verlag. 222-228.

Lynch, K. (1981): A theory of good city form. Cambridge, Mass.: MIT.
Lyotard, J.-F. (1979): La Condition postmoderne. Rapport sur le savoir. Paris: Minuit.
Lyotard, J.-F. (1983): Le Différend. Paris: Minuit.
Mach, E. (1906): Gedankenexperimente. In: Ibid: Erkenntnis und Irrtum. Skizzen zur Psychologie der Forschung. Vienna: Barth. 183–201.
McLuhan, M. (1964): Understanding Media. New York: McGraw Hill.
Meili, M. (2006): Zehn Behauptungen über Architektur und Wissenschaft. Beitrag Kolloquium Moravanski, ETH Zürich. Zurich: November 2006. http://www.meilipeter.ch/media/medialibrary/2013/07/2006_Zehn_Behauptungen_über_Architektur_und_Wissenschaft.pdf. Accessed: 10/29/2019.
Meili, M.; Wehrli-Schindler B.; Sevcik, T.; Eisinger, A.; Girsberger, E. (2011): Braucht Zürich visionäre Projekte? Panel discussion in the Stadthaus. Zurich: 01/13/2011.
Menand, L. (2001): The Metaphysical Club. London: Harper Collins.
Merleau-Ponty, M. (1966): Phänomenologie der Wahrnehmung. Berlin/New York: Walter de Gruyter.
Moneo, R. (2005): Theoretical Anxiety and Design Strategies in the Work of Eight Contemporary Architects. Cambridge, Mass.: MIT Press.
Moravánszky, A. (2015): Analogien und Attitüden. In: tec 21. Schweizerische Bauzeitung. No. 37/2015. 28–33.
Neumann, G. (2004): Die frühromantische Enzyklopädie. Novalis und sein Konzept des Wissenstheaters. In: Stammen, T.; Weber, W.: Wissenssicherung, Wissensordnung und Wissensverarbeitung. Das europäische Modell der Enzyklopädie. Berlin: Akademie.
Nerdinger, W. (Ed. 2003): Dinner for architects: Serviettenskizzen von berühmten Architekten. Munich: dva.
Novalis ([1799] 1968): Das Allgemeine Brouillon – Materialien zur Enzyklopädistik. In: Samuel, R: Novalis: Schriften. Die Werke Friedrich von Hardenbergs. Vol. 3. Das philosophische Werk II. Darmstadt: Wissenschaftliche Buchgesellschaft. 205–478.
Nyiri, K. (2004): Vernetztes Wissen. Vienna: Passagen.
Oechslin, W. (2012a): "Verwirklichung". Schinkels architektonisches Geschichtsverständnis. In: Schulze Altcappenberg, H.; Johannsen, R. (Eds.): Karl Friedrich Schinkel. Geschichte und Poesie. Das Studienbuch. Berlin: Deutscher Kunstverlag. 13–22.
Oechslin, W. (2012b): Der Architekt als Theoretiker. In: Nerdinger, W. (Ed.): Der Architekt. Geschichte und Gegenwart eines Berufsstandes. Munich: Prestel, Volume 2. 576–601.
Osborne, P. (2014): "Kunst" versus "Bild"? In: Texte zur Kunst 95 (September 2014). 48–55.
Ozbekhan, H. (1969): Toward a General Theory of Planning. In: Jantsch, E. (Ed.): Perspectives of Planning. Paris: OECD. 45–155.
Pehnt, W. (2011): Die Plangestalt des Ganzen. Der Architekt und Stadtplaner Rudolf Schwarz (1897–1961) und seine Zeitgenossen. Cologne: Verlag der Buchhandlung Walther König.
Peirce, C. S. ([1898] 1992): Reasoning and the Logic of Things. Cambridge: Cambridge University Press.
Peirce, C. S. ([1903] 1997): Pragmatism as a Principle and Method of Right Thinking: The 1903 Harvard Lectures on Pragmatism. New York: State University Press.
Peirce, C. S. (1929): Guessing. In: Hound and Horn 2(3). 267–282.
Peirce, C. S. (1958): The Collected Papers of Charles S. Peirce. Volumes 1–8. Cambridge, Mass.: Harvard University Press.
Peschken, G. (1979): Karl Friedrich Schinkel. Das architektonische Lehrbuch. Berlin: Deutscher Kunstverlag.
Pessoa, F. ([1933] 1991): Livro do desassosego. Volume 1+2. Lisbon: Preceça.
Plato ([360 B.C.] 2003): Timaios. Ditzingen: Reclam.
Plessner, H. ([1928] 1975): Die Stufen des Organischen und der Mensch, Einleitung in die philosophische Anthropologie. Berlin/New York: Walter de Gruyter.
Pfister, H. R.; Böhm, G. (2008): The multiplicity of emotions: A framework of emotional functions in decision making. In: Judgment and decision making, 3(1). 5–17.
Pfisterer, U. (Ed. 2011): Metzler-Lexikon Kunstwissenschaft. Ideen, Methoden, Begriffe. 2nd expanded and updated edition. Stuttgart: Metzler.
Polya, G. (1945): How to Solve It. Princeton: Princeton University Press.
Protzen, J.-P.; Harris, D. (2010): The Universe of Design. Horst Rittel's Theories of Design and Planning. London/New York: Routledge.
Reichertz, J. (1999): Gültige Entdeckung des Neuen? Zur Bedeutung der Abduktion in der qualitativen Sozialforschung. In: Österreichische Zeitschrift für Soziologie 24, 4. 47–64.

Rittel, H. (1992): Planen, Entwerfen, Design. Ausgewählte Schriften zu Theorie und Methodik. Stuttgart/Berlin/Cologne: Kohlhammer.

Rorty, R. (2007): Philosophy as Cultural Politics: Philosophical Papers. Cambridge: Cambridge University Press.

Rossi, A. ([1966] 1982): The Architecture of the City. Cambridge/London: MIT.

Rowe, C.; Koetter, F. (1984): Collage City. Cambridge, Mass.: MIT.

Ryle, G. (1949): The Concept of Mind. London: Hutchinson's University Library.

Safranski, R. (2007): Romantik. Eine deutsche Affäre. Munich: Hanser.

Salewski, C. (2012): Dutch New Worlds. Scenarios in Physical Planning and Design in the Netherlands, 1970-2000. Rotterdam: 010.

Salewski, C. (2014): Möglichkeitsräume. In: Professur Kees Christiaanse; Rieniets, T.; Kretschmann, N.; Perret, M.: Die Stadt als Ressource. Berlin: Jovis. 73-82.

Scamozzi, V. (1615): L'Idea della Architettura Universale. Venice.

Schleiermacher, F. ([1814] 1889): Dialektik. In: Ibid: Sämtliche Werke. Dritte Abteilung. Zur Philosophie. IV/2. Berlin: Reimer.

Schlögel, K. (2003): Im Raume lesen wir die Zeit. Über Zivilisationsgeschichte und Geopolitik. Munich: Carl Hanser.

Schön, D. (1983): The Reflective Practitioner: How Professionals Think in Action. New York: Basic.

Schön, D. (1985): The Design Studio: An Exploration of its Traditions & Potentials. London: RIBA.

Schön, D. (1987): Educating the Reflective Practitioner. San Francisco: Jossey-Bass.

Schön, D. (1988): Designing: Rules, types and worlds. In: Design Studies 9. 181-190.

Schön, D. (1992): Design as reflective conversation with the material. In: Research in Engineering Design 3. 131-147.

Schön, D.; Rein, M. (1994): Frame Reflection: Toward the Resolution of Intractable Policy Controversies. New York: Basic.

Schönwandt, W. (1986): Denkfallen beim Planen. Bauwelt-Fundamente, Volume 74. Braunschweig: Vieweg.

Schwarz, R. (1960): Kirchenbau. Welt vor der Schwelle. Heidelberg: Kerle.

Secchi, B.; Viganò, P. (2009): Antwerp, Territory of a New Modernity. Amsterdam: Sun.

Seel, M. (2007): Die Macht des Erscheinens. Frankfurt: Suhrkamp.

Semper, G. (1851): Die vier Elemente der Baukunst. Braunschweig: Vieweg.

Semper, G. (1860-1863): Der Stil in den technischen und tektonischen Künsten, oder Praktische Aesthetik: ein Handbuch für Techniker, Künstler und Kunstfreunde. Frankfurt a. M.: Verlag für Kunst und Wissenschaft.

Shane, D. G. (2005): Recombinant Urbanism: Conceptual Modeling in Architecture, Urban Design and City Theory. New York: Wiley.

Simon, H. (1962): The architecture of complexity. In: Proceedings of the American Philosophical Society, 106. 467-482.

Simon, H. (1973): The structure of ill-structured problems. In: Artificial Intelligence 4. 181-201.

Simpson, D. (2008): Performative Modernities: Rem Koolhaas's Delirious New York as inductive research. In: Swiss Federal Office of Culture (Ed.): Explorations in Architecture. Basel: Birkhäuser. 12-13.

Smith, M. K. ([2001] 2011): Donald Schön: Learning, reflection and change. The encyclopedia of informal education. www.infed.org/thinkers/et-schon.htm. Accessed: 10/29/2019.

Solà-Morales, M. de (1992): Periphery as Project. In: Ibid (2008): A Matter of Things. Rotterdam: NAi.

Solà-Morales, M. de (2008): A Matter of Things. Rotterdam: NAi.

Spector, T. (2001): The ethical architect. The dilemma of contemporary practice. New York: Princeton Architectural Press.

Spencer-Brown, G. (1969): Laws of Form. London: Allen and Unwin.

Stangl, W. (2018): Abduktion. Online Lexikon für Psychologie und Pädagogik. http:lexikon.stangl.eu/15/abduktion/. Accessed: 10/29/2019.

Stierli, M. (2010): Las Vegas im Rückspiegel. Die Stadt in Theorie, Fotografie und Film. Zurich: gta.

Taut, B. ([1935/36] 2009): Architekturüberlegungen. Architekturlehre. In: Arch +, No. 194. 36-157.

Toda, M. (1980): Emotion and decision making. In: Acta Psychologica, 45. 133-155.

Ungers, O. M.; Koolhaas, R.; Kollhoff, H.; Ovaska, A. ([1977] 2013): Die Stadt in der Stadt. In: Hertweck, F.; Marot, S. (Eds.): Die Stadt in der Stadt. Berlin: Ein Grünes Archipel. Kritische Ausgabe. Zurich: Lars Müller.

Ungers, O. M. (1980): Über das Denken und Entwerfen in Bildern und Vorstellungen. In: Architektur und Denkmalpflege 17. Sundermann, M; Lang, C.; Schwarz, M. (Eds.): Rudolph Schwarz. Düsseldorf/Bonn. 23.

Ungers, O. M. ([1981] 2011): Die Thematisierung der Architektur. Sulgen: Niggli.

Ungers, O. M. (1982): Morphologie. City Metaphors. Cologne: Verlag der Buchhandlung Walther König.
Ungers, O. M.; Koolhaas, R.; Obrist, H.-U. (2006): Die Rationalisierung des Bestehenden. Oswald Mathias Ungers im Gespräch mit Rem Koolhaas und Hans-Ulrich Obrist. In: Arch plus, No. 179. 6–11.
Valéry, P. ([1921]1973): Eupalinos oder die Architektur. Übertragen von Rainer Maria Rilke. Leipzig: Insel, 1927. Frankfurt: Suhrkamp.
Venturi, R. ([1966] 2003): Komplexität und Widerspruch in der Architektur. Basel/Boston/Berlin: Birkhäuser.
Venturi, R.; Scott Brown, D.; Izenour S. (1977): Learning from Las Vegas. Cambridge, Mass.: MIT.
Vester, F. (1999): Die Kunst vernetzt zu denken – Ideen und Werkzeuge für einen neuen Umgang mit Komplexität. Stuttgart: DVA.
Vignola, G. ([1562] 1600): Regola delli cinque Ordini d'Architettura. Amsterdam: Blaev.
Vitruvius ([approx. 33–22 B.C.] 1981): Zehn Bücher über Architektur. Darmstadt: Wissenschaftliche Buchgesellschaft.
Vogt, M.A. (1996): Le Corbusier, der edle Wilde. Braunschweig: Vieweg.
Van den Broeck, J. (2013): Balancing Strategic and Insitutional Planning: The Search for a Pro-Active Planning Instrument. In: disP – The Planning Review, 49:3. 43–47.
Von Foerster, H. (1993): Wissen und Gewissen: Versuch einer Brücke. Frankfurt: Suhrkamp.
Wilson, E. (1998): Consilience. The Unity of Knowledge. New York: Knopf.
Windelband, W. (1904): Geschichte und Naturwissenschaft. Strasbourg: Heitz.
Witt, H. (2004): Von der Marktforschung zur akademischen Lehre – eine ungewöhnliche Karriere. Gerhard Kleining im Interview mit Harald Witt. In: FQS (Forum Qualitative Sozialforschung), 5 (3), http://nbn-resolving.de/urn:nbn:de:0114-fqs0403404. Accessed: 10/29/2019.
Wittgenstein, L. (1921): Tractatus logico-philosophicus. Logisch-philosophische Abhandlung, in: Annalen der Naturphilosophie: Ostwald.

List of illustrations

Cover image: The author's own representation.
Figure 1: The author's own representation.
Figure 2: The author's own representation, after Horst Rittel.
Figure 3: The author's own representation, after Christian Gänshirt.
Figure 4: The author's own representation.
Figure 5, top: Robert Venturi, Denise Scott Brown, Steven Izenour. Courtesy of Venturi, Scott Brown and Associates.
Figure 5, bottom left: Rem Koolhaas, Zoe Zenghelis. Courtesy of Office for Metropolitan Architecture (OMA). Weena-Zuid 158, 3012 NC Rotterdam, The Netherlands. www.oma.com.
Figure 5, bottom right: Rem Koolhaas, Madelon Vriesendorp.
Figure 6: The author's own representation.
Figure 7, left: Robert Freno. Courtesy of Fondazione Aldo Rossi.
Figure 7, middle and right: Aldo Rossi. Courtesy of Fondazione Aldo Rossi.
Figure 8: Peter Eisenman. Courtesy of Eisenman Architects.
Figure 9, left: Manfred Brückels. https://commons.wikimedia.org/wiki/File:Shellhaus3a.jpg. Accessed: 11/16/2019.
Figure 9, right: Alfred Essa. https://www.flickr.com/photos/tatler/339218853/. Accessed: 11/16/2019.
Figure 10: Le Corbusier. Courtesy of Fondation Le Corbusier.
Figure 11: Christopher Alexander, Sara Ishikawa, Murray Silverstein. (1966): A Pattern Language. New York: Oxford University. 174, 177. Reproduced with permission of the Licensor through PLSclear.
Figure 12: Kevin Lynch (1984): Good City Form. Cambridge, Mass.: MIT. 286. Courtesy of MIT Press.
Figure 13: The author's own representation.
Figure 14: The author's own representation.
Figure 15: The author's own representation.

For their valuable discussions and help
I wish to thank:
Benno Agreiter, David Chipperfield,
Kees Christiaanse, Jörg H. Gleiter,
Arpad Hetey, Hans Hortig, Joris Jehle,
Matthias Löpfe, Daniel Kiss, Moritz
Köhler, Stefania Koller, Dorli and Robert
Kretz, Dimitri Kron, Felix Ledergerber,
Lino Moser, Christina Nater, Julia Rubin,
Christian Salewski, Matthias Sauerbruch,
Christian Schmid, Vera Schmidt,
Michael Stirnemann, Dominik Thurnherr,
Louis Wangler, Thorben Westerhuys,
Mirjam Züger and all students and
research colleagues with whom I was able
to learn, research and teach about *the
cognitive potential of design* during my work
at ETH Zurich and at the University
of Zurich.

Special thanks to the Professorship for
Architecture and Urban Design Prof. em.
Kees Christiaanse, the Departments of
Architecture and of Civil, Environmental
and Geomatic Engineering at ETH Zurich,
the Center for Urban & Real Estate
Management at the University of Zurich,
the Swiss National Science Foundation
and The Rolex Mentor and Protégé
Arts Initiative.

Imprint

© 2020 Simon Kretz and
Verlag der Buchhandlung Walther König,
Cologne

English translation
  Kenneth Friend

English copy editing
  Claire Cahm

Graphic concept and design
  Joris Kritis with Bernardo Rodrigues

Paper
  Splendorlux Pearl Ice, Munken Pure

Lithography, printing and binding
  Lösch GmbH & Co. KG

First published by
  Verlag der Buchhandlung Walther König,
  Cologne
  Ehrenstr. 4
  D – 50672 Cologne
  Tel.: +49 (0) 221 / 20 59 6 53
  verlag@buchhandlung-walther-koenig.de

Distribution
  Germany, Austria, Switzerland/Europe
  Buchhandlung Walther König
  Ehrenstr. 4
  D – 50672 Cologne
  Tel: +49 (0) 221/20 59 6 53
  verlag@buchhandlung-walther-koenig.de

  UK & Ireland
  Cornerhouse Publications Ltd. – HOME
  2 Tony Wilson Place
  UK – Manchester M15 4FN
  Tel.: +44 (0) 161 212 3466
  publications@cornerhouse.org

  Outside Europe
  D.A.P./Distributed Art Publishers, Inc.
  75 Broad Street, Suite 630
  USA – New York, NY 10004
  Tel.: +1 (0) 212 627 1999
  enadel@dapinc.com

ISBN 978-3-96098-734-5

All rights reserved. No part of this publication may be produced, stored in a retrieval system or transmitted in any form or by any means, electronic, mechanical, photocopying, recording or otherwise, without the prior permission of the publisher.

We thank all holders of image usage rights for the friendly consent to publication.
If, despite intensive research, a holder of rights should not have been taken into consideration, we ask them to contact the publishing house. Any missing information will be corrected and supplemented in subsequent editions. Justified claims will be covered in the context of the usual agreements.

Further publications of Simon Kretz:

Daniel Kiss and Simon Kretz (2020, Eds.)
Relational Theories of Urban Form. An Anthology
Birkhäuser Verlag, Basel

Simon Kretz and David Chipperfield (2018, Eds.)
On Planning – A Thought Experiment
Verlag der Buchhandlung Walther König, Cologne

Christian Salewski and Simon Kretz (2017)
An Assemblage of Assemblers: The 2006 Antwerp Strategic Structural Plan s-RSA
In: disP the Planning Review 208 – Vol. 53.1 (1/2017)

Simon Kretz and Lukas Kueng (2016, Eds.)
Urbane Qualitäten. Ein Handbuch am Beispiel der Metropolitanregion Zürich
Edition Hochparterre, Zurich

Simon Kretz and Christian Salewski (2014)
Urbanity of Things
In: Rieniets, T. et al. (Eds.): The City as Resource
jovis Verlag, Berlin

Simon Kretz (2014)
Narration. Storytelling as an Urban Design Tool
In: Rieniets, T. et al. (Eds.): The City as Resource
jovis Verlag, Berlin